AA

CENTRAL ASSESSMENT KIT

Technician Unit 11

Drafting Financial Statements

In this August 2000 edition

- Thorough, reliable updating of material to 1 August 2000 taking into account changes in accounting standards and guidance

- Many additional central assessment questions

FOR DECEMBER 2000 AND JUNE 2001 CENTRAL ASSESSMENTS

BPP Publishing
August 2000

First edition 1998
Third edition August 2000

ISBN 0 7517 6243 1 (Previous edition 0 7517 6175 3)

British Library Cataloguing-in-Publication Data
A catalogue record for this book
is available from the British Library

Published by

BPP Publishing Limited
Aldine House, Aldine Place
London W12 8AW

www.bpp.com

Printed in England by W M Print
Frederick Street
Walsall
West Midlands WS2 9NE

We are grateful to the Lead Body for Accounting for permission to reproduce extracts from the Standards of Competence for Accounting.

Page

INTRODUCTION

(v)

How to use this Central Assessment Kit – Central Assessment
Technique - Unit 11 Standards of Competence - Assessment Strategy

Questions   *Answers*

QUESTIONS AND ANSWERS

The headings indicate the main topics of questions, but questions often cover several different topics.

A date (6/96, say) after the question title refers to the central assessment set under the previous version of the standards.

Contents

HOW TO USE THIS CENTRAL ASSESSMENT KIT

Aims of this Central Assessment Kit

> To provide the knowledge and practice to help you succeed in the central assessment for Technician Unit 11 *Drafting Financial Statements (Accounting Practice, Industry and Commerce)*.

To pass the central assessment you need a thorough understanding in all areas covered by the standards of competence.

> To tie in with the other components of the BPP Effective Study Package to ensure you have the best possible chance of success.

Interactive Text
This covers all you need to know for central assessment for Unit 11 *Drafting Financial Statements*. Icons clearly mark key areas of the text. Numerous activities throughout the text help you practise what you have just learnt.

Central Assessment Kit
When you have understood and practised the material in the Interactive Text, you will have the knowledge and experience to tackle this Central Assessment Kit for Unit 11. It contains the AAT's December 1999 Central Assessment for Unit 11 plus relevant questions from the AAT's Specimen Central Assessment and central assessments set under the previous version of the Standards.

RECOMMENDED APPROACH TO THIS CENTRAL ASSESSMENT KIT

- To achieve competence in all units, you need to be able to do **everything** specified by the standards. Study the text very carefully and do not skip any of it.

- Learning is an **active** process. Do **all** the activities as you work through the text so you can be sure you really understand what you have read.

- After you have covered the material in the Interactive Text, work through this **Central Assessment Kit**.

  The Kit is made up of three different types of question:

  - **Practice questions** are designed to help you practise techniques in particular areas of the Standards at a lower level than you will experience in the central assessments themselves. They are 'warm-ups' which you may find it particularly useful to do if it is some time since you studied the Interactive Text and the activities it contains. The questions contain guidance notes which lead you through how to tackle the answer. The answers are preceded by tutorial notes which highlight tricky points in the question.

  - **Full central assessment standard questions** give you plenty of practice in the type of question that comes up in the central assessment. Many are taken from central assessments set by the AAT under the previous version of the Standards. All have full answers with tutorial notes.

  - The AAT's **December 1999 Central Assessment** for the Unit with full answers provided by BPP.

- The structure of the main body of this Central Assessment Kit follows that of its companion Interactive Text, with banks of both practice and full central assessment standard questions for each area of the Standards. You may opt to do all the practice questions from across the range of the Standards first, or you may prefer to do questions of both levels in a particular area of the Standards before moving on. In either case, it is probably best to leave the December 1999 Central Assessment until the last stage of your revision, and then attempt it as a 'mock' under 'exam conditions'. This will help you develop some key techniques in selecting questions and allocating time correctly. For guidance on this, please see **Central Assessment Technique** on page (vii).

- This approach is only a suggestion. You college may well adapt it to suit your needs.

Remember this is a **practical** course.

- Try to relate the material to your experience in the workplace or any other work experience you may have had.

- Try to make as many links as you can to your study of the other Units at this level.

CENTRAL ASSESSMENT TECHNIQUE

Passing central assessments at this level is half about having the knowledge, and half about doing yourself full justice on the day. You must have the right **technique**.

The day of the central assessment

1 Set at least one **alarm** (or get an alarm call) for a morning central assessment

2 Have **something to eat** but beware of eating too much; you may feel sleepy if your system is digesting a large meal

3 Allow plenty of **time to get to where you are sitting the central assessment**; have your route worked out in advance and listen to news bulletins to check for potential travel problems

4 **Don't forget** pens, pencils, rulers, erasers

5 Put **new batteries** into your calculator and take a spare set (or a spare calculator)

6 **Avoid discussion** about the central assessment with other candidates outside the venue

---

Technique in the central assessment

1 *Read the instructions (the 'rubric') on the front of the paper carefully*

Check that the format of the paper hasn't changed. It is surprising how often assessors' reports remark on the number of students who attempt too few questions. Make sure that you are planning to answer the **right number of questions**.

2 *Select questions carefully*

Read through the paper once - don't forget that you are given 15 minutes' reading time - then quickly jot down key points against each question in a second read through. Select those questions where you could latch on to 'what the question is about' - but remember to check carefully that you have got the right end of the stick before putting pen to paper. Use your 15 minutes' reading time wisely.

3 *Plan your attack carefully*

Consider the **order** in which you are going to tackle questions. It is a good idea to start with your best question to boost your morale and get some easy marks 'in the bag'.

4 *Check the time allocation for each section of the paper*

Time allocations are given for each section of the paper. When the time for a section is up, you must go on to the next section. Going even one minute over the time allowed brings you a lot closer to failure.

5 *Read the question carefully and plan your answer*

Read through the question again very carefully when you come to answer it. Plan your answer to ensure that you **keep to the point**. Two minutes of planning plus eight minutes of writing is virtually certain to earn you more marks than ten minutes of writing.

BPP PUBLISHING

6   *Produce relevant answers*

Particularly with written answers, make sure you **answer the question set,** and not the question you would have preferred to have been set.

7   *Gain the easy marks*

Include the obvious if it answers the question, and don't try to produce the perfect answer.

Don't get bogged down in small parts of questions. If you find a part of a question difficult, get on with the rest of the question. If you are having problems with something, the chances are that everyone else is too.

8   *Produce an answer in the correct format*

The assessor will state *in the requirements* the format in which the question should be answered, for example in a report or memorandum.

9   *Follow the assessor's instructions*

You will annoy the assessor if you ignore him or her. The **assessor will state** whether he or she wishes you to 'discuss', 'comment', 'evaluate' or 'recommend'.

10   *Lay out your numerical computations and use workings correctly*

Make sure the layout fits the **type of question** and is in a style the assessor likes.

Show all your **workings** clearly and explain what they mean. Cross reference them to your answer. This will help the assessor to follow your method (this is of particular importance where there may be several possible answers).

11   *Present a tidy paper*

You are a professional, and it should show in the **presentation of your work.** Students are penalised for poor presentation and so you should make sure that you write legibly, label diagrams clearly and lay out your work neatly. Markers of scripts each have hundreds of papers to mark; a badly written scrawl is unlikely to receive the same attention as a neat and well laid out paper.

12   *Stay until the end of the central assessment*

Use any spare time **checking and rechecking** your script.

13   *Don't worry if you feel you have performed badly in the central assessment*

It is more than likely that the other candidates will have found the assessment difficult too. Don't forget that there is a competitive element in these assessments. As soon as you get up to leave the venue, **forget** that central assessment and think about the next - or, if it is the last one, celebrate!

14   *Don't discuss a central assessment with other candidates*

This is particularly the case if you **still have other central assessments to sit.** Even if you have finished, you should put it out of your mind until the day of the results. Forget about assessments and relax!

UNIT 11 STANDARDS OF COMPETENCE

The structure of the Standards for Unit 11

The Unit commences with a statement of the **knowledge and understanding** which underpin competence in the Unit's elements.

The unit of Competence is then divided into **elements of competence** describing activities which the individual should be able to perform.

Each element includes:

- A set of **performance criteria** which define what constitutes competent performance

- A **range statement** which defines the situations, contexts, methods etc in which competence should be displayed

- **Evidence requirements**, which state that competence must be demonstrated consistently, over an appropriate time scale with evidence of performance being provided from the appropriate sources

- **Sources of evidence**, being suggestions of ways in which you can find evidence to demonstrate that competence. These fall under the headings: 'observed performance; work produced by the candidate; authenticated testimonies from relevant witnesses; personal account of competence; other sources of evidence'.

The elements of competence for Unit 11: *Drafting Financial Statements (Accounting Practice, Industry and Commerce)* are set out below. Knowledge and understanding required for the unit as a whole are listed first, followed by the performance criteria, range statements and evidence requirement for each element.

Unit 11: Drafting Financial Statements (Accounting Practice, Industry and Commerce)

What is the unit about?

The unit is concerned with assessing the ability of candidates to interpret and understand the structure and purpose of financial statements from various organisations. It requires the candidate to analyse the financial statements of limited companies using ratio analysis and to draft limited company, sole trader and partnership year-end financial statements from a trial balance.

Unit 11 is assessed by an unseen Central Assessment. Guidance on the sort of tasks covered in the central assessment are set out in the Assessment Strategy.

Unit 11 Standards of Competence

Knowledge and understanding

The business environment

- An awareness of the elements and purposes of financial statements of different types of organisation (Element 11.1)

- The requirements of the legislative and regulatory framework (Elements 11.1 & 11.2)

- General legal framework of limited companies, partnerships and sole traders: types of limited companies, obligations of directors, partners and sole traders in respect of the accounts (Element 11.2)

- Forms of equity and loan capital (Element 11.2)

- Main requirements of relevant SSAPs, FRSs and other relevant pronouncements and their application to this element (Element 11.2)

- Statutory form of accounting statements: disclosure requirements (Element 11.2)

- The presentation of corporation tax in financial statements (Element 11.2)

- The need to prepare accounts and statements in proper form (Element 11.2)

Accounting techniques

- Form and method of preparation of financial statements (Element 11.2)

- Methods of analysing and interpreting the information contained in financial statements (Elements 11.1 & 11.2)

- Application of the general principles of consolidation (Element 11.2)

- Computing and interpreting accounting ratios (Elements 11.1 & 11.2)

Accounting principles and theory

- Differences between the published accounts of different types of organisations (Element 10.1)

- Generally accepted accounting principles and concepts (Elements 11.1 & 11.2)

The organisation

- Understanding that the accounting systems of an organisation are affected by its roles, organisational structure, its administrative systems and procedures and the nature of its business transactions (Elements 11.1 & 11.2)

Element 11.1   Interpret financial statements

Performance criteria

1   The general purpose of financial statements used in various organisations is identified

2   Elements in financial statements used in various organisations are identified

3   The relationship of elements within financial statements is identified

4   The relationship between elements of limited company financial statements is interpreted

5   Unusual features or significant issues are identified within financial statements

6   Valid conclusions are drawn from the information contained within financial statements

7   Conclusions and interpretations are clearly presented

Range statement

1   Financial statements: balance sheet; income statement

2   Elements: assets; liabilities; ownership interest; income; expenditure contribution from owners; distribution to owners; gains and losses

3   Relationship between elements: profitability; liquidity; efficient use of resources; financial position

Element 11.2   Draft limited company, sole trader and partnership year end financial statements

Performance criteria

1   Financial statements are accurately drafted from the appropriate information

2   Subsequent adjustments are correctly implemented

3   Draft accounts comply with domestic standards and legislation and, where relevant, partnership agreement

4   A cash flow statement is correctly prepared and interpreted where required

5   Year end financial statements are presented for approval to the appropriate person in a clear form

6   Confidentiality procedures are followed at all times

7   The organisation's policies, regulations, procedures and timescales relating to financial statements are observed at all times

8   Discrepancies, unusual features or queries are identified and either resolved or referred to the appropriate person

Range statement

1   Financial statements: profit and loss account; balance sheet; owner's capital and current account; cash flow statement; statement of total recognised gains and losses; the supplementary notes required by statute, SSAPs, FRSs or other relevant pronouncements

2   Domestic standards: relevant SSAPs; relevant FRSs; other relevant pronouncements

3   Limited company financial statements: unitary; consolidated

ASSESSMENT STRATEGY

This unit is assessed by *central assessment* only.

A central assessment is a means of collecting evidence that you have the **essential knowledge and understanding** that underpins competence. It is also a means of collecting evidence across the **range of contexts** for the standards and evidence of your ability to transfer skills, knowledge and understanding to different situations. Thus, although central assessments will contain practical tasks linked to the performance criteria, they will also focus on the underpinning knowledge and understanding. You should in addition expect each central assessment to contain tasks taken from across a broad range of the Standards.

The Central Assessment will last for 3 hours (plus 15 minutes reading time) and will be divided into two sections. Section 1 will comprise 30% of the total assessment and will address Element 11.1 only. Section 2 will comprise 70% of the assessment and address Element 11.2 only.

Element 11.1 will be assessed in **Section 1**. Typical tasks might include the following.

- Setting out the general purpose of financial statements and illustrating this by identifying the users of financial statements in various organisations and their needs.

- Identifying and explaining the nature of the elements of financial statements.

- Explaining what is meant by the balance sheet equation and how the elements fit into the equation.

- Demonstrating awareness of the nature of the ownership interest in profit-making organisations (capital) and in public sector and not-for-profit organisations (fund balances).

- Contrasting the ownership interest in a profit-making organisation with that in a public sector or not-for-profit organisation.

- Demonstrating understanding of the structure of profit and loss accounts and income and expenditure accounts.

- Explaining the articulation of the income statement with the balance sheet.

- Applying ratio analysis to company financial statements and analysing and interpreting the results, including comparison with industry averages, for various purposes.

Element 11.2 will be assessed in **Section 2**.

Typical tasks in the section concerned with drafting limited company financial statements might include the following.

- Making adjustments using journal entries to the balances in an extended trial balance in accordance with the requirements of company law, accounting concepts, and FRSs and SSAPs.

- Explaining the reasons for the adjustments by reference to company law, accounting concepts, and FRSs and SSAPs.

- Drafting a profit and loss account and/or balance sheet of a company from an extended trial balance in accordance with the format and requirements of company law and accounting standards.

- Setting out and explaining the reporting requirements of companies under company law.

- Demonstrating a knowledge of the standard-setting process.

- Drafting a consolidated profit and loss account and/or balance sheet using the financial statements of parent and subsidiary undertakings in accordance with company law and accounting standards.

- Drafting notes to the accounts as required by law and accounting standards.

- Drafting a statement of total recognised gains and losses.

- Drafting a reconciliation of movements in shareholders' funds and a note of historical cost profits and losses.

- Drafting a cash-flow statement and a reconciliation between cash flow from operating activities and operating profit from information in the balance sheets, profit and loss account and additional information provided.

Typical tasks in the section concerned with drafting sole trader or partnership financial statements might include:

- Making adjustments using journal entries to the balances in an extended trial balance for sole traders and/or partnerships in accordance with the requirements of accounting concepts and generally accepted accounting principles.

- Explaining the reasons for the adjustments by reference to accounting concepts and generally accepted accounting principles.

- Setting out the genera legal framework of sole traders and/or partnerships and the obligations in respect of accounts.

- Drafting a profit and loss account and/or balance sheet of a sole trader and /or partnership from an extended trial balance.

- Drawing up an appropriation account for a partnership.

- Preparing partners' current and capital accounts, including entries relating to the admission and retirement of partners and to the dissolution of the partnership.

Questions

1 OBJECTIVES (25 mins)

(a) State the objectives of financial reporting.

(b) Identify the various groups of users of a financial reporting package.

(c) Discuss the information needs of any two of the groups of users identified above.

(d) Discuss the following statement: 'The diverse information needs of the various user groups cannot be fully met by the current financial reporting package used by companies?'.

2 FUNDAMENTAL (25 mins)

Financial reporting is based upon a number of fundamental concepts.

(a) Identify and explain the four fundamental concepts referred to by SSAP 2.

(b) Explain and give an example of a conflict which may exist between the fundamental concepts when they are applied.

(c) The ASB *Statement of Principles* (Chapter 2) refers to the qualitative characteristics of financial information. State and explain the primary characteristics which make financial information useful.

3 ASSETS (25 mins)

(a) Explain the following terms:

Fixed asset
Current asset
Current liability

(b) Under what circumstances should a fixed asset be recognised in the financial statements of an entity?

(c) Explain how items which have been hired by a business should be recognised in the financial statements.

4 ORGANISATION (25 mins)   12/98

(a) State one type of profit-making and one type of public sector or not-for-profit organisation.

For each type of organisation:

(i) Give an example of an external user of the financial statements.

(ii) Describe one type of decision which would be made by the users with the assistance of the financial statements of the organisation.

(b) The accounting equation is often expressed as:

$$\text{ASSETS} - \text{LIABILITIES} = \text{OWNERSHIP INTEREST}$$

(i) Explain what each of the terms 'assets', 'liabilities' and 'ownership interest' means.

(ii) Identify, in general terms only, the balances that would appear in the 'ownership interest' section of the balance sheet of one profit-making and one public sector or not-for-profit organisation.

5 PRIMARY FINANCIAL STATEMENTS (25 mins)

(a) Identify the primary financial statements which a business produces.

(b) Explain the links between the primary financial statements.

(c) Discuss the relevance of the primary financial statements to a large charitable organisation (constituted as a limited company).

(d) Discuss the extent to which the primary financial statements produced by a business will satisfy the information needs of a member of the public.

6 OBJECTIVE AND ELEMENTS (20 mins)   Specimen

(a) What is the objective of financial statements?

(b) Illustrate how this objective is fulfilled by considering the financial statements of one type of profit-making body and one type of public sector or not-for-profit organisation.

(c) Identify the elements of financial statements.

(d) Explain how the elements are related in the balance sheet and in the profit and loss account of a profit-making organisation and the relationship between the two financial statements.

(e) What major difference would you expect to find in the balance sheet of a public sector or not-for-profit organisation when compared with that of a profit-making organisation?

7 PRACTICE QUESTION: COUNTRY CRAFTS

Country Crafts Ltd is a small business started in 20W9. It buys in craft items, for example, pottery, hand-made clothes and wooden toys from a large number of small craft producers, and then sells them to craft shops throughout the country.

The rented premises consist of a warehouse containing racks and bins to hold the craft products along with an adjoining office and garage. The company owns two delivery vans, used for both collections and deliveries, and two company cars.

The company was started by two friends, Sandip Patel and Abdul Mohim, who met on a small business training course in Leicester. Sandip has responsibility for buying and selling and has built up a network of small craftworkers who make stock for him. Abdul is responsible for the running of the warehouse and the office and the administration of the business.

In addition to the two owners, the business employs two drivers, a warehouseman, two accounts clerks and a secretary.

You are the senior of the two accounts clerks and you are responsible for the nominal ledger.

The company's accounts are currently operated using a manual system, but computerisation of the accounts should take place in the near future and some equipment has recently been purchased.

The sales ledger holds at present about 100 accounts; the company has no cash customers.

All purchases of craft products are on credit and the purchase ledger contains about 80 accounts.

There are very few cash transactions. Any that do occur, for example, window cleaning, office sundries and travel expenses, are dealt with by a simple petty cash system. A £50 float is maintained, expenditure is recorded in a simple petty cash book and at irregular intervals the expenditure is posted to the nominal ledger.

Depreciation policy

Rates:			
	Motor vehicles	25% pa	straight line
	Office furniture	10% pa	straight line
	Computer equipment	33 1/3% pa	straight line

Depreciation is charged a full year in the year of purchase and is not charged for in the year of sale.

Zero scrap values are assumed.

Fixed asset information

Motor vehicles:

Delivery vans	H247AFE	K174RFU
Date of purchase	9.8.X0	12.8.X2
Cost	£16,200	£19,800

Company cars	J168TFE	J169TFE
Date of purchase	11.9.X1	11.9.X1
Cost	£9,200	£9,200

Office furniture:

All office furniture was purchased upon incorporation of the business on 1 September 1989.

Cost	£4,850

Computer equipment:

Date of purchase	1 June 20X3
Cost	£16,830

Mark-up policy

The company marks up all its products by 100% on cost.

Further information

(a)   Listed below is the company's trial balance at 31 December 20X3.

COUNTRY CRAFTS LIMITED
TRIAL BALANCE AS AT 31 DECEMBER 20X3

	Dr £	Cr £
Motor vans (cost)	36,000	
Motor cars (cost)	18,400	
Office furniture (cost)	4,850	
Computer equipment (cost)	16,830	
Motor vans (provision for dep'n)		17,100
Motor cars (provision for dep'n)		9,200
Office furniture (provision for dep'n)		1,940
Computer equipment (provision for dep'n)		
Stock	24,730	
Debtors control	144,280	
Bank		610
Cash	50	
Creditors control		113,660
Sales		282,490
Purchases	152,140	
Rent	12,480	
Heat and light	1,840	
Wages and salaries	75,400	
Office expenses	7,900	
Motor expenses	14,890	
Depreciation (motor vans)		
Depreciation (office furniture)		
Depreciation (computer equipment)		
Share capital		50,000
Profit and loss		35,850
VAT		12,640
Suspense	13,700	
	523,490	523,490

(b) Adjustments need to be made for the following.

(i) On 2 December 20X3 a new delivery van, L673NFU, was purchased for £22,600. Van H247AFE was given in part exchange, the balance of £17,600 being paid for by cheque and debited to the suspense account.

(ii) On 4 December 20X3, as a cost-saving measure, company car J168TFE was sold for £3,900 and the receipt credited to the suspense account.

(iii) On 20 December 20X3 the company had allowed a local organisation to use its car park and adjacent field for a Car Boot Sale. For this service the company was paid £250.00. This amount had been credited to the sales account.

(c) The following additional matters need to be taken into account.

(i) Depreciation for the year ended 31 December 20X3 is to be provided for.

(ii) On 15 December 20X3 a rack full of china craft products fell in the warehouse. These products, valued at £2,300 at selling price, were so badly damaged that they had to be thrown away. The Raven Moon Insurance Company have agreed to compensate for the damage except for the first £200. A claim has been submitted, but so far no payment has been received.

(iii) The stocktake on 30 December 20X3 revealed stock at cost price of £31,640.

Two batches of stock, however, were of particular note:

(1) a batch of Baby Beatrice mugs, value at selling price £320, were judged to be saleable for only £120;

(2) a batch of Windsor Fire Damage plates, value at selling price £620, were judged to be saleable for only £350.

(iv) Several small customers had been going out of business recently, probably because of the recession. The company's accountant had therefore judged it prudent to create a provision for doubtful debts representing 5% of the trade debtors figure at the year end.

(v) Petty cash transactions for December were as follows.

December 3	Window cleaning	£10.00
December 8	Tea and coffee	£4.40
December 12	Xmas decorations	£28.60
December 20	Petty cash float replenished	£50

These transactions, including the withdrawal from the bank, have not yet been entered into the company's books.

(vi) The electricity bill for the September, October, November quarter for £315 had been received on 16 December and entered into the purchase ledger. It is normal for the electricity bill for the December, January, February quarter to be double that for the previous quarter.

(vii) The rent of £7,488 per annum is paid annually in advance on 1 September.

Tasks

(a) Prepare journal entries for the transactions listed in (b) above using the journal provided on page 8. Narratives are required.

(b) Enter all the account balances, including those adjusted in Task (a), in the first two columns of the extended trial balance on page 9.

(c) Make appropriate entries in the adjustment columns of the extended trial balance.

(d) Extend the figures into the extended trial balance columns for profit and loss account and balance sheet. Total all columns, transferring the balance of profit or loss as appropriate.

Guidance notes

1   This question is a revision of your studies of the extended trial balance at intermediate level, where you were mainly concerned with sole traders.

2   Make sure that you have fully mastered the principles of the ETB before you attempt the questions on the ETB and partnerships or limited companies.

BPP PUBLISHING

JOURNAL		Page 20
Details	**DR** £	**CR** £

JOURNAL		Page 20

	LEDGER BALANCES		ADJUSTMENTS		PROFIT AND LOSS A/C		BALANCE SHEET BALANCES	
	DEBIT	CREDIT	DEBIT	CREDIT	DEBIT	CREDIT	DEBIT	CREDIT
	£	£	£	£	£	£	£	£
Motor vans (cost)								
Motor cars (cost)								
Office furniture (cost)								
Computer equipment (cost)								
Motor vans (prov for dep'n)								
Motor cars (prov for dep'n)								
Office furniture (prov for dep'n)								
Computer equipment (prov for dep'n)								
Stock								
Debtors control								
Bank								
Cash								
Creditors control								
Sales								
Purchases								
Rent								
Heat and light								
Wages and salaries								
Office expenses								
Motor expenses								
Dep'n (motor vans)								
Dep'n (motor cars)								
Dep'n (office furniture)								
Dep'n (computer equipment)								
Share capital								
Profit and loss								
VAT								

BPP PUBLISHING

8 TAYLORIANA (36 mins)

You have been approached by Samuel Taylor, a sole trader who runs a small trading company, Tayloriana (distributing catering equipment) for help in producing year-end financial statements. He employs a part-time bookkeeper who has produced an extended trial balance for the business as at 31 March 20X5. Samuel is negotiating to enter into an existing partnership, Coleridge & Co, which operates in the same area of activity as his own. The existing partners of Coleridge & Co would like to see the latest profit figures of Samuel's business. You have been asked to assist in the preparation of a profit and loss account for the year ended 31 March 20X5.

The extended trial balance of Tayloriana as at 31 March 20X5 is set out on page 10.

Samuel Taylor has given you the following further information.

(a) Stock has been counted on 31 March 20X5. The cost of stock calculated on a first in first out basis is £49,300. The selling price of the stock is estimated at £65,450.

(b) After the year end, one of the debtors, whose year-end balance was £2,500, went into liquidation. The liquidator has stated that there will be no assets available to repay creditors. No provision for this bad debt has been made in the accounts and the balance is still included in year-end debtors.

Tasks

(a) Draft a profit and loss account for Tayloriana for the year ended 31 March 20X5 incorporating any adjustments which may be required as a result of the further information set out above.

(b) Explain to Samuel Taylor any adjustments you have made by reference to applicable accounting standards.

TAYLORIANA LIMITED
EXTENDED TRIAL BALANCE 31 MARCH 20X5

Description	Trial balance Debit £	Trial balance Credit £	Adjustments Debit £	Adjustments Credit £	Profit and loss account Debit £	Profit and loss account Credit £	Balance sheet Debit £	Balance sheet Credit £
Drawings	21,500						21,500	
Lighting and heating	1,760				1,760			
Purchases	162,430				162,430			
Sales		257,350				257,350		
Sales ledger control account	41,000						41,000	
Fixtures and fittings (cost)	28,000						28,000	
Motor vehicles (cost)	16,500						16,500	
Bad debts	540				540			
Returns outwards		7,460				7,460		
Capital 1.4.X4		44,080						44,080
Stock 1.4.X4	43,700				43,700			
Rent, rates and insurance	8,500		300	150	8,650			
Accumulated depreciation: fixtures and fittings		12,000		2,800				14,800
Accumulated depreciation: motor vehicles		6,300		4,100				10,400
Bank charges	320				320			
Cash at bank and in hand	1,800						1,800	
Purchase ledger control account		47,200						47,200
Depreciation: fixtures and fittings			2,800		2,800			
Depreciation: motor vehicles			4,100		4,100			
Carriage inwards	1,320				1,320			
Returns inwards	3,350				3,350			
Postage, stationery and telephone	2,910				2,910			
Wages	39,420				39,420			
Carriage outwards	850				850			
Prepayments			150				150	
Accruals				300				300
Discounts allowed	490				490			
Loss for the year						7,830	7,830	
	374,390	374,390	7,350	7,350	272,640	272,640	116,780	116,780

9 SANDRO VENUS (45 mins)

You have been asked by Sandro Venus to assist in the preparation of the year end financial statements of his business. He is a sole trader who runs a trading business which specialises in ornaments decorated with sea shells. The extended trial balance as at 31 March 20X7 is set out on the next page.

You are given the following further information.

(a) A general provision for doubtful debts is to be set up at 5% of the year end debtors' balance.

(b) During the year Sandro Venus took goods which had cost £500 for his own personal use in decorating his flat.

(c) At the end of the year, one of the motor vehicles which had cost £5,500 and on which there was accumulated depreciation of £2,400 was sold for £3,500. Payment for the vehicle sold has not yet been received by Sandro Venus and no entry to reflect the sale has been made in the extended trial balance.

Tasks

(a) Make any additional adjustments you feel necessary to the balances in the extended trial balance as a result of the matters set out in the further information above. Set out your adjustments in the form of journal entries.

Note. Narratives are not required.

(b) Draft a profit and loss account for the year ended 31 March 20X7.

(c) Sandro Venus is considering whether to incorporate the business and has said that he will telephone you tomorrow for advice.

Prepare notes for the telephone conversation that will enable you to explain the difference between the legal status of a sole trader and that of a company in respect of :

(i) The liability of the owners for the debts of the business
(ii) The legal identity of the business
(iii) The regulation of the production of financial statements for the business

SANDRO VENUS
EXTENDED TRIAL BALANCE 31 MARCH 20X7

DESCRIPTION	TRIAL BALANCE Debit £	Credit £	ADJUSTMENTS Debit £	Credit £	PROFIT AND LOSS Debit £	Credit £	BALANCE SHEET Debit £	Credit £
Wages and National Insurance Contributions	28,996		348		29,344			
Capital as at 1 April 20X6		83,696						83,696
Postage and stationery	524				524			
Accumulated depreciation - motor vehicles		8,125		6,094				14,219
Accumulated depreciation - office equipment		1,375		1,375				2,750
Accumulated depreciation - fixtures & fittings		2,780		2,780				5,560
Purchases	103,742				103,742			
Trade creditors		17,725						17,725
Carriage inwards	923				923			
Motor vehicles (cost)	32,500						32,500	
Office equipment (cost)	13,745						13,745	
Fixtures & fittings (cost)	27,800						27,800	
Sales		187,325				187,325		
Returns outwards		1,014				1,014		
Trade debtors	18,740						18,740	
Drawings	14,400						14,400	
Depreciation - motor vehicles			6,094		6,094			
Depreciation - office equipment			1,375		1,375			
Depreciation - fixtures & fittings			2,780		2,780			
Prepayments			320				320	
Accruals				1,131				1,131
Stock	27,931		30,229	30,229	27,931	30,229	30,229	
Returns inwards	1,437				1,437			
Cash at bank	9,473						9,473	
Cash in hand	166						166	
Bank deposit interest		972				972		
Carriage outwards	657				657			
Rent, rates and insurance	8,041			320	7,721			
Bad debts	830				830			
Discounts allowed	373				373			
Bank charges	693				693			
Telephone	3,524		783		4,307			
Lighting and heating	3,755				3,755			
Motor expenses	4,762				4,762			
Profit					22,292			22,292
	303,012	303,012	41,929	41,929	219,540	219,540	147,373	147,373

10 JONATHAN BROWN (27 mins) 6/96

You have been asked to advise Jonathan Brown, a sole trader, on the accounting treatment of certain transactions which he feels might affect his financial statements for the year ended 31 December 20X5. The matters on which he would like your advice are set out below.

(a) The business paid for an advertising campaign during the year at a cost of £2,800. It is estimated by Jonathan Brown that this will lead to an overall increase in sales of 15%. Half of this increase was achieved in 20X5 and the other half is expected to be achieved in 20X6.

(b) Jonathan Brown took stock costing £500 from the business at the end of the year for his own use. He removed the stock on 31 December 20X5 after the year-end stock count had taken place. No adjustment was made to the stock balance to take account of this action.

(c) During the year a word processor, which had a written down value of £850, was accidentally dropped out of the window during an office party and destroyed. The asset has been written out of the books of the business. The insurance company has refused to meet the cost of the loss. The solicitors of the business are currently pursuing the matter through the courts and say that the company has a reasonable chance of success.

(d) Jonathan Brown has put his own house up as security for a loan made by the bank to his business. The loan was made specifically for the business and not for the personal use of Jonathan Brown.

Advise Jonathan Brown on the accounting treatment of these transactions in his financial statements for the year ended 31 December 20X5. Explain your treatment, where relevant, by reference to accounting concepts and generally accepted accounting principles.

11 LOCKE, BERKELEY AND HUME (55 mins) 12/98

Jack Locke, Jane Berkeley and Sreela Hume were in partnership together selling and distributing scientific equipment. On 1 October 20X7 they admitted Bhatti Ayer into the partnership. You have been asked to finalise the partnership accounts for the year ended 30 September 20X8 and to make the entries necessary to account for the admission of Bhatti into the partnership. You have been given the following information.

(a) On 1 October 20X7 Bhatti paid £50,000 into the partnership. The profit-sharing ratios in the old partnership were:

Jack   5/12
Jane   4/12
Sreela 3/12

The new profit-sharing ratios are now:

Jack   5/15
Jane   4/15
Sreela 3/15
Bhatti 2/15

On the day that Bhatti was admitted to the partnership, the goodwill in the partnership was valued at £180,000. No goodwill is to be kept in the accounts of the new partnership. Adjustments for goodwill are to be made in the capital accounts of the partners.

(b) Jack has produced a set of accounts which shows a profit of £164,100 for the year ended 30 September 20X8.

On further enquiry you discover that one of the debtors, who had owed the business £12,500, had gone into liquidation during the year to 30 September 20X8 and the liquidators have said that there are no funds available to meet creditor balances. No adjustment has yet been made for this item.

An invoice for £4,200 was received on 13 November 20X8 relating to delivery costs of equipment sold to customers during the year to 30 September 20X8. It had not been included in the accounts as it had been received after the year end.

(c) Interest on capital is to be paid at a rate of 10% on the balance at the year end on the capital accounts. No interest is paid on the current accounts.

(d) Cash drawings in the year amounted to:

Jack £48,200
Jane £39,300
Sreela £29,800
Bhatti £25,400

(e) The partners are entitled to the following salaries per annum.

Jack £15,000
Jane £12,000
Sreela £8,000
Bhatti £8,000

(f) The balances on the current and capital accounts at the beginning of the year, before any adjustments had been made for the admission of Bhatti into the partnership, were as follows.

Capital accounts		*Current accounts*	
Jack	£37,000	Jack	£5,300
Jane	£31,000	Jane	£4,200
Sreela	£26,000	Sreela	£3,100

Tasks

(a) Produce a statement adjusting the profit figure given to you by Jack, taking into account the matters set out above, and calculate the net profit figure for the appropriation.

Note. You do not need to set out your adjustments in the form of journal entries.

(b) Justify any adjustments made to the profit figure in part (a) by referring, where relevant, to accounting concepts.

(c) Prepare the partners' capital accounts for the year ended 30 September 20X8.

(d) Prepare an appropriation account for the partnership for the year ended 30 September 20X8.

(e) Prepare the partners' current accounts for the year ended 30 September 20X8.

You have been asked by Middlemarch and Co, a partnership, to attend a meeting of the partners at which they will agree the year end accounts. The partnership has a book-keeper who has kept the books and produced a profit and loss account for the partnership, but he requires some assistance to produce the final financial statements for the year ended 31 March 20X4. You have had a preliminary meeting with the bookkeeper and have made notes of the information given as follows.

(a)   The original partners of Middlemarch and Co were Brooke, Featherstone and Lydgate. They shared profits and losses in the following proportions: Brooke five-tenths, Featherstone three-tenths and Lydgate two-tenths.

(b)   On 1 April 20X3, Mary Garth was admitted to the partnership. She agreed to introduce £8,000 in cash into the business. It was agreed that the new profit-sharing ratios were to be as follows.

Brooke	four-tenths
Featherstone	three-tenths
Lydgate	two-tenths
Garth	one-tenth

(c)   At 1 April 20X3, goodwill was valued at £30,000. No account for goodwill is to be maintained in the books of the partnership, but adjusting entries in respect of goodwill are to be made in the capital accounts of the partners.

(d)   Mary Garth is to receive a salary of £6,000. Lydgate already receives a salary of £5,000 and this is to be continued.

(e)   Partners are to receive interest on their capital accounts of 10% per annum on the balance outstanding at the end of the year. No interest is to be allowed on the balances of current accounts.

(f)   The balances on the capital and current accounts at 1 April 20X3 were as follows.

	Capital	*Current*
	£	*£*
Brooke	20,000	4,500 CR
Featherstone	14,000	3,800 CR
Lydgate	9,000	1,800 DR

(g)   In addition to her balance on the capital account, Brooke has loaned the partnership £8,000. She is entitled to interest on this loan at a rate of 8% per annum.

(h)   The partners' drawings during the year were as follows.

	£
Brooke	19,320
Featherstone	16,100
Lydgate	14,300
Garth	13,600

(i)   The net profit for the year to 31 March 20X4 as calculated by the bookkeeper before taking into account partners' salaries and interest due was £56,740.

The partners have asked the bookkeeper a number of questions about the year end accounts which he is unable to answer. They have therefore asked you to answer their questions.

Tasks

(a) Draw up the appropriation account for the partnership of Middlemarch and Co for the year ended 31 March 20X4. (20 mins)

(b) Prepare the partners' current and capital accounts for the year ended 31 March 20X4, recording therein the entries necessary upon the introduction of Mary Garth into the partnership. (20 mins)

(c) Answer the following questions which the partners have asked about the year end accounts. Justify your answers, where appropriate, by reference to accounting concepts, SSAPs and/or FRSs.

(i) We noted that, in preparing the accounts for the year, a debtor balance of £4,600 was written off as a bad debt, thus reducing profit by that amount. We understand that the debtor concerned had gone into liquidation after the year end and that we did not know that the debt would not be recoverable until after 31 March 20X4. Why did we not wait until next year to write off the debt since that is when the debtor went into liquidation?

(ii) The partnership is currently engaged in a legal case in which we are being sued for damages amounting to £53,000 arising out of a contract. Our lawyers claim that we have a very good defence to the claim and, in their opinion, it is unlikely that any damages will have to be paid. Can we ignore this claim for the purposes of our year end financial statements?

(iii) We understand that you wish to make an adjustment in the year end accounts in respect of goodwill arising out of the admission of a new partner to the partnership. Why is any adjustment necessary? Would any of the existing partners be disadvantaged if no adjustment was made in the accounts for goodwill?

(iv) Is there any need for our partnership agreement to be altered in the light of the balances on the current account at the end of the year?

(14 mins)

13 SHIPS (50 mins) **6/99**

Mary Rose, Nelson Victory and Elizabeth Second are in partnership together hiring out river boats. Mary has decided to retire from the partnership at the end of the day on 31 March 20X9. You have been asked to finalise the partnership accounts for the year ended 31 March 20X9 and to make the entries necessary to account for the retirement of Mary from the partnership on that day.

You have been given the following information.

(a) The profit for the year ended 31 March 20X9 was £106,120.

(b) The partners are entitled to the following salaries per annum.

Mary	£18,000
Nelson	£30,000
Elizabeth	£13,000

(c) Interest on capital is to be paid at a rate of 12% on the balance at the beginning of the year on the capital accounts. No interest is paid on the current accounts.

(d) Cash drawings in the year amounted to:

Mary   £38,000
Nelson   £30,000
Elizabeth   £29,000

(e) The balances on the current and capital accounts at 1 April 20X8 were as follows.

Capital accounts		*Current accounts*	
Mary	£28,000 Cr	Mary	£2,500 Cr
Nelson	£26,000 Cr	Nelson	£2,160 Cr
Elizabeth	£22,000 Cr	Elizabeth	£1,870 Cr

(f) The profit-sharing ratios in the partnership are currently:

Mary   4/10
Nelson   3/10
Elizabeth   3/10

On the retirement of Mary, Nelson will put a further £40,000 of capital into the business. The new profit-sharing ratios will be:

Nelson   6/10
Elizabeth   4/10

(g) The goodwill in the partnership is to be valued at £90,000 on 31 March 20X9. No separate account for goodwill is to be maintained in the books of the partnership. Any adjusting entries in respect of goodwill are to be made in the capital accounts of the partners.

(h) The partners have had the assets of the partnership valued at 31 March 20X9. The book value of the assets at that date and the valuation are as follows.

	Book value £	*Valuation* £
Land and buildings	278,000	328,000
Debtors	36,000	26,000

The valuations are to remain in the books of the new partnership.

(i) Any amounts to the credit of Mary on the date of her retirement should be transferred to a loan account.

Tasks

(a) Prepare the partners' capital accounts as at 31 March 20X9 showing the adjustments that need to be made on the retirement of Mary from the partnership.

(b) Prepare an appropriation account for the partnership for the year ended 31 March 20X9.

(c) Prepare the partners' current accounts for the year ended 31 March 20X9.

(d) Show the balance on Mary's loan account as at 31 March 20X9.

(e) Draft a letter to the partners explaining briefly, and giving reasons for, the adjustments that you have made to the capital accounts of the partners on the retirement of Mary from the partnership on 31 March 20X9.

14   **ALICE, BONNY AND CLYDE (45 mins)**

You have been approached by a partnership, Alice, Bonny and Clyde, to prepare their accounts for the year ending 31 October 20X4. You have established that profit available for appropriation is £78,000 for the year and have been given the following information.

(a)   Originally only Alice and Bonny were in partnership, sharing profits in a ratio of 2:1. On 1 November 20X3 they admitted the third partner, Clyde. Clyde contributed capital of £10,000 on 1 November 20X3. The new profit sharing ratio is 3:2:1 to Alice, Bonny and Clyde respectively.

(b)   Goodwill was valued at £30,000 on 1 November 20X3 and this must be taken into account when admitting Clyde; goodwill is not to be kept in the accounts. The profit sharing ratio to be used on elimination of the goodwill is 3:2:1 to Alice, Bonny and Clyde respectively.

(c)   Interest on capital is paid at a rate of 10% based on the year-end capital amount. No interest is allowed on the balance of current accounts.

(d)   Drawings made for the year ending 31 October 20X4 were:

	£
Alice	38,000
Bonny	19,500
Clyde	15,000

(e)   Alice is entitled to a salary of £10,000 per annum, and Clyde is entitled to £5,000 per annum.

(f)   You have been supplied with the balance sheet of the partnership as at 31 October 20X3.

BALANCE SHEET OF ALICE AND BONNY AS AT 31 OCTOBER 20X3

	£	£
Fixed assets		
Motor cars	20,000	
Fixtures and fittings	4,000	
		24,000
Current assets		
Stock	8,000	
Debtors	3,500	
	11,500	
Current liabilities		
Creditors	2,000	
Bank overdraft	3,000	
	5,000	
Net current assets		6,500
Total assets less current liabilities		30,500
Represented by:		
Capital accounts		
Alice	14,000	
Bonny	10,000	
		24,000
Current accounts		
Alice	4,000	
Bonny	2,500	
		6,500
		30,500

Tasks

(a) Based on the above information, draw up an appropriation account for the partnership of Alice, Bonny and Clyde for the year ended 31 October 20X4.

(b) Prepare the partners' current and capital accounts for the year ended 31 October 20X4 showing clearly the effect of admitting Clyde to the partnership.

15   COLERIDGE (36 mins)   12/95

Samuel Taylor has a number of questions about his decision to enter into partnership with Coleridge & Co which he would like your help to answer. He has obtained the latest balance sheet of the partnership. The simplified balance sheet of the partnership Coleridge & Co as at 30 June 20X5 is set out below.

		£
Fixed assets		240,000
Net working capital		120,000
		360,000
	£	
Partners' capital accounts		
Wordsworth	138,000	
Quincey	65,000	
Southey	84,000	
		287,000
Partners' current accounts		
Wordsworth	35,000	
Quincey	18,000	
Southey	20,000	
		73,000
		360,000

The terms of the proposed entry of Samuel Taylor into the partnership are set out as follows.

(a) On the entry of Samuel Taylor into the partnership, Wordsworth will retire. Samuel will pay £80,000 of capital in cash into the partnership.

(b) Under the existing partnership agreement the three partners share profits in the following ratios.

Wordsworth	5/10
Quincey	3/10
Southey	2/10

When Samuel Taylor joins the partnership the new profit sharing ratio will be:

Quincey	4/10
Southey	3/10
Taylor	3/10

(c) As part of the retirement arrangements the fixed assets of the old partnership will be revalued to £340,000. Goodwill has been estimated at £50,000 and the accounts will be adjusted to reflect this fact on the retirement of Wordsworth. Goodwill is to be eliminated in the books of the new partnership and so no goodwill account will be maintained.

(d) The balance on the capital account of Wordsworth is to be transferred to a loan account and will be repaid in two years' time.

Tasks

(a) Make the necessary entries in the capital accounts of the partners to reflect the retirement of Wordsworth and the admission of Samuel Taylor into the partnership of Coleridge & Co in accordance with the provisions set out above, assuming that the entry was made on 30 June 20X5.

(b) Samuel Taylor has asked the following questions concerning his proposed entry into the partnership of Coleridge & Co. Provide answers for him.

    (i) What is goodwill and why is it necessary to make an adjustment for goodwill on the retirement of a partner?

    (ii) What are the advantages of conducting business as a partnership rather than as a sole trader? (Name *two* examples.)

16   STOOGE (45 mins)   6/96

You have been asked to take over work on finalising the accounts of the partnership of Stooge & Co. An extended trial balance for the year ended 31 March 20X6 has already been produced and is set out on page 22.

You are given the following further information.

(a) Mo was admitted into the partnership on 1 April 20X5. Before he entered the partnership the profit-sharing ratio was as follows.

                       Curly   6/10
                       Larry   4/10

After the admission of Mo into the partnership the profit-sharing ratio became:

                       Curly   5/10
                       Larry   3/10
                       Mo   2/10

(b) Goodwill was valued at £60,000 at the time of admission of Mo into the partnership. An adjustment for goodwill should have been made in the accounts of the partnership on the admission of Mo, but this has yet to be done. Although goodwill must be taken into account, no balance of goodwill is to be kept in the final accounts of the partnership.

(c) No adjustment has yet been made for interest on capital. The partnership deed states that interest is to be allowed on the balance of the capital accounts of the partners at the end of the year at a rate of 10%.

Tasks

(a) Prepare an appropriation account for the partnership, starting with the balance of net profit in the profit and loss appropriation account on the extended trial balance.

(b) Prepare the partners' current and capital accounts for the year ended 31 March 20X6 from the balances in the extended trial balance, taking into account the further information provided above.

STOOGE & CO
EXTENDED TRIAL BALANCE AS AT 31 MARCH 20X6

Description	Trial balance Debit £'000	Trial balance Credit £'000	Adjustments Debit £'000	Adjustments Credit £'000	Profit and loss a/c Debit £'000	Profit and loss a/c Credit £'000	Profit and loss appropriation a/c Debit £'000	Profit and loss appropriation a/c Credit £'000	Balance sheet Debit £'000	Balance sheet Credit £'000
Motor vehicles - cost	61								61	
Office equipment - cost	14								14	
Purchases	199				199					
Cash at bank	26								26	
Sales		382				382				
Debtors	79								79	
Stock	28		33	33	28	33			33	
Expenses	36		8	6	38					
Drawings: Curly	30								30	
Larry	24								24	
Mo	32								32	
Motor vehicles - accumulated depreciation		20								20
Office equipment - accumulated depreciation		6								6
Creditors		19								19
Accruals				8						8
Current accounts: Curly		6								6
Larry	4								4	
Capital accounts: Curly		40								40
Larry		20								20
Mo		40								40
Prepayments			6						6	
Net profit					150			150		
Partners' salaries: Curly							30			30
Larry							20			20
Mo							20			20
Balance of net profit							80			80
	533	533	47	47	415	415	150	150	309	309

BPP PUBLISHING

17   PRIDE (70 mins)

You have been asked by Pride and Co, a partnership, to assist in the preparation of the financial statements for the year ended 31 October 20X6 and to give advice on partnership matters. From your initial discussions with the bookkeeper you have constructed a summarised profit and loss account which is set out below.

PRIDE AND CO
PROFIT AND LOSS ACCOUNT FOR THE YEAR ENDED 31 OCTOBER 20X6

	£
Sales	600,000
Cost of sales	360,000
Gross profit	240,000
Expenses	150,000
Net profit	90,000

You have obtained the following information about the partnership of Pride and Co.

(a)   The partners of Pride and Co are Jane, Elizabeth and Lydia. They share profits and losses in the following proportions.

Jane	five-tenths
Elizabeth	three-tenths
Lydia	two tenths

(b)   Jane receives a salary of £15,000, Elizabeth a salary of £10,000 and Lydia a salary of £5,000.

(c)   Partners receive interest on their capital accounts of 8% per annum on the balance outstanding at the end of the year. No interest is to be allowed on the balances of current accounts.

(d)   The balances on the capital and current accounts at 1 November 20X5 were as follows.

	Capital £	Current £
Jane	25,000	5,700 CR
Elizabeth	22,000	4,200 CR
Lydia	3,000	2,300 DR

There were no injections or withdrawals of capital by the partners during the year to 31 October 20X6.

(e)   Jane, in addition to her balance on the capital account, has loaned the partnership £10,000. She is entitled to interest on this loan at a rate of 10% per annum.

(f)   The partners' drawings during the year were as follows.

	£
Jane	15,600
Elizabeth	14,700
Lydia	18,900

The partners have been negotiating with Asmah, a sole trader, with a view to admitting her as a partner on 1 November 20X6. If Asmah is admitted into the partnership she will bring into it as her capital contribution the net assets of her business at a fair value of £35,000. She will bring with her the existing customers of her business. Her summarised profit and loss account for the year ended 31 October 20X6 is set out below.

ASMAH
PROFIT AND LOSS ACCOUNT FOR THE YEAR ENDED 31 OCTOBER 20X6

	£
Sales	200,000
Cost of sales	110,000
Gross profit	90,000
Expenses	70,000
Net profit	20,000

(a) If Asmah is admitted into the partnership an adjustment for goodwill, which is currently not shown as an asset in the books of the partnership, is to be made in the books of Pride and Co.

(b) Goodwill has been valued at £60,000.

(c) No account for goodwill will be maintained in the books of the new partnership. Any adjustment affecting the partners is to be made in the capital accounts of the partners.

(d) An adjustment will have to be made in order to reflect the fair values of the assets in the existing partnership. The fixed assets of the partnership are currently included in the books of the partnership at a net book value of £88,000. The current market value of the assets is £128,000. Any adjustment affecting the partners is to be made in the capital accounts of the partners.

In the new partnership the profit sharing ratios will be as follows.

Jane	five-twelfths
Elizabeth	three-twelfths
Lydia	two-twelfths
Asmah	two-twelfths

Tasks

(a) Draw up the appropriation account for the partnership of Pride and Co for the year ended 31 October 20X6.

(b) Write a report to the existing partners of Pride and Co covering the following matters.

 (i) Using appropriate profitability ratios, compare the performance of the existing partnership of Pride and Co with that of Asmah. On the basis of your calculations and any other matters you consider relevant, advise the existing partners on the desirability of admitting Asmah into the partnership.

 Note. You can assume that a similar level of sales, cost of sales and expenses will be achieved in the next financial year.

 (ii) What legal formalities would you recommend as a result of the admission of a new partner into the business?

 (iii) Show what entries would have to be made in the capital accounts of the partnership if, taking into account your advice, the partnership were to go ahead and admit Asmah into the partnership on 1 November 20X6.

18 GRACES (25 mins) 6/97

You are required to attend a meeting of the partners Alice Grace, Ethel Grace and Isabella Grace. They are three sisters who are in partnership together selling gardening equipment. They share profits in the ratio:

Alice	5/12
Ethel	4/12
Isabella	3/12

They will admit a fourth partner, Flora Bundi, into the business on 1 June 20X7. She will put £30,000 into the partnership. The profit sharing ratios will then become:

Alice	4/10
Ethel	3/10
Isabella	2/10
Flora	1/10

You have been given the following additional information.

(a) The business has freehold land and buildings which had originally cost £120,000 and on which, at 31 May 20X7, there is accumulated depreciation of £25,000. The land and buildings have recently been re-valued at £179,000.

(b) Motor vehicles which had originally cost £24,000 and on which, at 31 May 20X7, there is accumulated depreciation of £8,400 are now thought to be worth only £6,000.

(c) The new values of the freehold and buildings and the motor vehicles are to be incorporated into the partnership on admission of the new partner with any adjustment being made in the capital accounts of the partners.

(d) Goodwill has been valued at £144,000 and it has been agreed to adjust the capital balances of the partners to reflect the goodwill that exists in the business. A goodwill account is to be maintained in the new partnership.

The capital account balances for the existing partnership at 31 May 20X7 are as follows:

	£
Alice	55,000
Ethel	45,000
Isabella	40,000

Tasks

(a) Make the necessary entries in the capital accounts of the partners to reflect the admission of Flora into the partnership on 1 June 20X7 taking into account the terms of entry given in the information supplied above.

(b) Draft notes to take to the meeting to explain why adjustments to the partners' capital accounts are necessary to take into account the new value of the land and buildings and the motor vehicles.

19 AMANDA BLAKE (35 mins) Specimen

Amanda Blake, John Turner, Sheila Cotman and Fred Reynolds are in partnership together as wholesale distributors of prints of popular paintings. Amanda has produced a draft profit and loss account for the partnership for the year ended 31 December 1997 and has asked you to finalise the partnership accounts. She has given you the following information that is relevant to the year in question.

(a) Interest on capital is to be paid at a rate of 10% on the balance at the year end on the capital accounts. No interest is paid on the current accounts.

(b) Cash drawings in the year amounted to:

Amanda	£51,000
John	£38,000
Sheila	£36,000
Fred	£24,000

(c) The partners are entitled to the following salaries per annum:

Amanda	£14,000
John	£11,000
Sheila	£9,000
Fred	£8,000

(d) On 1 January 1997, the partners admitted Fred Reynolds into the partnership. He paid £45,000 cash into the partnership on that date. The profit-sharing ratios in the old partnership were:

Amanda	4/10
John	3/10
Sheila	3/10

The new profit-sharing ratios are now:

Amanda	4/12
John	3/12
Sheila	3/12
Fred	2/12

On the day that Fred was admitted into the partnership, the goodwill in the partnership was valued at £156,000. No goodwill is to be kept in the accounts of the new partnership. Adjustments for goodwill are to be made in the capital accounts of the partners.

(e) The balances on the current and capital accounts at the beginning of the year, before any adjustments have been made for the admission of Fred into the partnership, were as follows.

Capital accounts:

Amanda	£36,600
John	£31,200
Sheila	£25,200

Current accounts:

Amanda	£4,200
John	£3,600
Sheila	£2,700

(f) The net profit per the accounts given to you by Amanda amounted to £151,800.

Tasks

(a) Prepare the partners' capital accounts for the year ended 31 December 20X7 from the information provided above.

(b) Prepare an appropriation account for the partnership for the year ended 31 December 1997.

(c) Prepare the partners' current accounts for the year ended 31 December 1997.

20 BLUTHER (70 mins)

A partnership, Bluther and Co, has asked you to assist its bookkeeper in the finalisation of its accounts for the year ended 31 March 20X8. You have had an initial meeting with the bookkeeper and have established the following information.

(a) The net profit for the year to 31 March 20X8 is calculated by the bookkeeper as being £75,500 before taking into account any appropriations.

(b) The original partners of Bluther and Co are Bothina and Luther. They shared profits equally until 1 April 20X7 when a third partner, Edwina, was admitted. Edwina agreed to introduce £20,000 in cash into the business on admission. It was also agreed that the new profit-sharing ratio would be as follows.

Bothina	2/5
Luther	2/5
Edwina	1/5

(c) On 1 April 20X7 goodwill was valued at £50,000. No account for goodwill is to be maintained in the books of the partnership, but adjusting entries in respect of goodwill are to be made in the capital accounts of the partners.

(d) Bothina receives a salary of £8,000 per annum, and Edwina receives a salary of £5,000 per annum.

(e) The partners receive interest of 10% per annum on the year end balance of their capital accounts. No interest is paid on current accounts.

(f) The balances on the capital and current accounts on 1 April 20X7 were as follows.

Partner	Capital account	Current account
	£	£
Bothina	20,000	5,000
Luther	15,000	3,000

(g) In addition to his balance on the capital account, Luther has loaned the partnership £10,000 at a rate of interest of 12% per annum. This has not been charged against the net profit figure.

(h) The partners' drawings during the year were as follows.

Partner	Drawings
	£
Bothina	10,000
Luther	12,000
Edwina	8,000

Tasks

(a) Prepare the partners' capital accounts for the year ended 31 March 20X8, recording the entries necessary upon the introduction of Edwina into the partnership.

(b) Draw up the appropriation account for the partnership for the year ended 31 March 20X8.

(c) Prepare the partners' current accounts for the year ended 31 March 20X8.

(d) The partners have asked you to answer a number of questions which are outlined below. Draft a short memo to the partners answering the questions.

    (i) During the year ended 31 March 20X8, a bad debt was written off for a company whose liquidator was appointed on 7 April 20X8. Would it not be more appropriate to write that particular bad debt off in the year ended 31 March 20X9?

(ii)   What is goodwill and why should it be adjusted in the accounts on the admission of a new partner?

(iii)   Should assets and liabilities be revalued on the admission of a new partner and, if so, why?

21   FINALISE (70 mins)   12/98

A partnership has approached you to help finalise its accounts. Its bookkeeper has prepared the profit and loss account for the year ended 30 September 20X8.

(a)   The profit amounts to £56,000 before the deduction of interest on the loan from Henry (one of the partners) and any appropriations of profit.

(b)   Until 1 October 20X7 there were three partners sharing profits/losses as follows.

Thomas	2/5
Gina	2/5
Henry	1/5

(c)   On 1 October 20X7 Alex was admitted, bringing £25,000 cash into the partnership. At that date goodwill was valued at £80,000. No account for goodwill is to be maintained in the books of the partnership, but adjusting entries in respect of goodwill are to be made in the capital accounts of the partners.

(d)   From 1 October 20X7 all four partners share profits and losses equally.

(e)   Thomas receives a salary of £7,000 per annum, and Henry receives a salary of £5,000 per annum.

(f)   The partners receive interest on their capital accounts of 10% per annum on the year end balance. No interest is paid on current accounts but interest is charged on drawings and the following amounts are to be charged for the year ended 30 September 20X8.

	£
Thomas	1,200
Gina	1,100
Henry	1,300
Alex	1,000

(g)   The balances on the capital and current accounts on 1 October 20X7 were as follows.

Partner	Capital account £	Current account £
Thomas	10,000	2,000
Gina	15,000	4,000
Henry	12,000	1,000

(h)   In addition to his balance on the capital account, on 1 October 20X7 Henry loaned the partnership £5,000 at a rate of interest of 12% per annum.

(i)   The partners' drawings during the year ended 30 September 20X8 were as follows.

Partner	Drawings £
Thomas	12,000
Gina	11,000
Henry	13,000
Alex	10,000

Tasks

(a) Prepare the partners' capital accounts for the year ended 30 September 20X8, recording the entries necessary upon the introduction of Alex into the partnership.

(b) Draw up the appropriation account for the partnership for the year ended 30 September 20X8.

(c) Prepare the partners' current accounts for the year ended 30 September 20X8.

(d) The partners have asked you to answer a number of questions which are outlined below. Reply in a short memo to the partners.

(i) Stock includes items which cost the partnership £10 each but would realise £15 now. Could the stock items be valued at £15 each?

(ii) The partners are considering converting their partnership to a limited company. How would their liability as partners in a partnership differ from the liability of shareholders in a limited company?

22 PRACTICE QUESTION: DEPRECIATION

Explain briefly the provisions of FRS 15 *Tangible fixed assets* where:

(a) An asset is disposed of
(b) The method of depreciating assets is changed

Guidance notes

1   In part (a) you should try to think carefully whether the provisions of the FRS 3 have any relevance here.

2   Part (b) is more difficult to explain in words than to apply in practice!

23 PRACTICE QUESTION: STOCKS

Statement of Standard Accounting Practice No 9 states that stocks and work in progress, other than long-term contract work in progress, should be valued at the 'lower of cost and net realisable value'. You are required to define the meaning of:

(a) Cost
(b) Net realisable value

Guidance notes

1   A very straightforward question, particularly if you have a good memory!

2   You should know these definitions very well as you will almost certainly be asked to apply them to a practical problem.

3   A 'memory test' such as this may well come up as part of a longer task. It is an easy way of demonstrating your competence, and you would be advised to do it first to give yourself confidence.

24 SSAP 13 (50 mins)

SSAP 13 *Accounting for research and development* defines certain categories of research and development expenditure. The standard also lays down rules which must be applied to the capitalisation of research and development expenditure.

Tasks

(a) List and explain the categories of expenditure.   (10 mins)

(b) Explain the criteria applied to research and development expenditure, according to SSAP 13, to determine whether the cost should be capitalised. (27 mins)

(c) Discuss briefly why there was a need for a SSAP relating to research and development expenditure. (13 mins)

25   FUN (50 mins)   12/98

You have been asked to assist in the preparation of the financial statements of Fun Ltd for the year ended 30 September 20X8. The company is a distributor of children's games. You have been provided with the extended trial balance of Fun Ltd as at 30 September 1998, which is set out on page 31.

You have been given the following further information.

(a) The share capital of the business consists of ordinary shares with a nominal value of 25 pence.

(b) The company has paid an interim dividend of 6 pence per share this year and is proposing a final dividend of 10 pence per share.

(c) Depreciation has been calculated on all of the fixed assets of the business and has already been entered into the distribution costs and administrative expenses ledger balances as shown on the extended trial balance.

(d) The corporation tax charge for the year has been calculated as £972,000.

(e) Interest on the loan has been paid for the first eleven months of the year only, but no interest has been paid or charged for the final month of the year. The loan carries a rate of interest of 8% per annum of the balance outstanding on the loan.

Tasks

(a) Make any additional adjustments you feel to be necessary to the balances in the extended trial balance as a result of the matters set out in the further information above. Set out your adjustments in the form of journal entries.

Notes

1   Narratives and dates are not required.
2   Ignore any effect of these adjustments on the tax charge for the year as given above.

(b) Taking account of any adjustments made in Part (a), draft a profit and loss account for the year ended 30 September 20X8 using Format 1 in accordance with the Companies Act 1985 as supplemented by FRS 3 *Reporting financial performance*.

You are *not* required to produce note to the accounts.

(c) The directors are interest in expanding operations next year. They wish to be clear about the constituents of the equity on the balance sheet and on the impact that leasing equipment, rather than purchasing equipment, might have on the company's balance sheet. They would like you to attend the next meeting of the Board.

FUN LIMITED

EXTENDED TRIAL BALANCE AS AT 30 SEPTEMBER 20X8

	Trial balance		Adjustments		Profit and loss account		Balance sheet	
	Debit £'000	Credit £'000	Debit £'000	Credit £'000	Debit £'000	Credit £'000	Debit £'000	Credit £'000
Trade debtors	2,863						2,863	
Bank overdraft		316						316
Interest	300				300			
Profit and loss account		3,811						3,811
Provision for doubtful debts		114						114
Distribution costs	2,055		614		2,669			
Administrative expenses	1,684		358		2,042			
Returns inwards	232				232			
Sales		14,595				14,595		
Land – cost	2,293						2,293	
Buildings – cost	2,857						2,857	
Fixtures and fittings – cost	1,245						1,245	
Motor vehicles – cost	2,524						2,524	
Office equipment – cost	872						872	
Stock	1,893		2,041	2,041	1,893	2,041	2,041	
Purchases	6,671				6,671			
Interim dividend	480				480			
Trade creditors		804						804
Buildings – accumulated depreciation		261		51				312
Fixtures and fittings – accumulated depreciation		309		124				433
Motor vehicles – accumulated depreciation		573		603				1,176
Office equipment – accumulated depreciation		184		81				265
Prepayments	63						63	
Carriage inwards	87				87			
Returns outwards		146				146		
Accruals				113				113
Investments	2,244						2,244	
Loan		3,600						3,600
Ordinary share capital		2,000						2,000
Share premium		1,300						1,300
Revaluation reserve		350						350
Profit					2,408			2,408
TOTAL	28,363	28,363	3,013	3,013	16,782	16,782	17,002	17,002

Prepare notes to bring to the Board meeting dealing with the following matters.

(i) How the balances on the share premium and the revaluation reserve arose.

(ii) The recommendation of one of the directors is to lease the assets as he says that this means that the asset can be kept off the balance sheet. Comment on this recommendation.

26 WOODPECKER (80 mins)   6/94

You are working in the business services department of a firm of accountants. A client of the firm, Woodpecker Ltd, a wholesale builders' merchant, has recently lost its financial accountant and has asked the firm to provide assistance in drafting the financial statements of the company for the year ended 31 March 20X4. The accountant who left the company has produced an extended trial balance, which includes some of the normal year end adjustments, and gathered some further information which may be relevant to the year end accounts. You have been asked by one of the partners of the firm to take on the task.

The extended trial balance of Woodpecker Ltd is set out on page 34. The following further information is provided.

(a) The authorised share capital of the company is as follows.

4,000,000 ordinary shares of 25p each
500,000 10% preference shares of £1.00 each

At the beginning of the year 1,600,000 shares were in issue (all were fully paid). A further 800,000 shares were issued during the year at a price of 75p per share. The whole of the proceeds of the issue, which were received in full, was credited to the ordinary share capital account.

(b) The directors decided that instead of paying a dividend to ordinary shareholders they would make a bonus issue of shares at the year end. Ordinary shareholders received one ordinary share of 25p for every six ordinary shares held by them at the year end. No entries have been made in the extended trial balance to reflect this issue.

(c) The interim dividend in the trial balance represents a dividend paid to preference shareholders. It has been decided to provide for the full preference dividend in the yearend accounts but no entry has yet been made to reflect this decision.

(d) No interest on the debentures has been paid during the year or provided for in the extended trial balance.

(e) The investment property shown in the extended trial balance at a value of £800,000 represents an office building purchased by the company as an investment. It has been revalued by J Wheeler and Co, a firm of chartered surveyors, at £600,000 based on its value given its current use. The valuation has not been reflected in the extended trial balance.

(f) Audit fees of £25,000 have not been paid or provided for in the extended trial balance.

(g) The corporation tax charge for the year has been calculated as £275,000.

(h) The balance on the goodwill account arose out of the purchase of an unincorporated business some years ago. The goodwill was purchased at a cost of £50,000 and is being amortised over ten years. No entry has been made for the amortisation of goodwill for the year ended 31 March 20X4.

(i) The remuneration of the directors for the year was as follows.

	£
Chairman	31,000
Sales director	42,000
Executive director	56,000

The remuneration of the directors is included in the salaries and wages figure in the extended trial balance. The directors' fees and pension contributions made on behalf of the directors are made up as follows.

	Fees	*Pension contributions*
	£	£
Chairman	2,000	4,000
Sales director	2,000	5,000
Executive director	3,000	6,000
	7,000	15,000

The two directors other than the sales director work on general administration.

(j) For the purposes of the published financial statements the following allocation of expenses is to be made.

	Distribution costs £'000	*Administrative expenses* £'000
Motor expenses	47	31
Light and heat	20	6
Insurance	29	9
General expenses	186	48
Depreciation of motor vehicles	151	38
Depreciation of office equipment	22	15
Depreciation of buildings	16	5
Depreciation of fixtures and fittings	65	-

Salaries and wages, excluding directors' remuneration, are to be allocated on the basis of 75% to the distribution department and 25% to the administration department.

(k) All the operations of the company are continuing operations.

Tasks

(a) Make any adjustments you feel to be necessary to the balances in the extended trial balance as a result of the matters set out in the further information above. Set out your adjustments in the form of journal entries. (Ignore any effect of these adjustments on the tax charge for the year as given above.) (16 mins)

No narratives are required for the journal entries.

(b) (i) Draft a profit and loss account for the year ended 31 March 20X4 and a balance sheet as at that date in a form suitable for publication using Format 1 in accordance with the Companies Act 1985 as supplemented by FRS 3 Reporting financial performance. (Students are not required to prepare a statement of total recognised gains and losses or the reconciliation of movements in shareholders' funds required under FRS 3.)

(ii) Provide suitable notes to the accounts, in so far as the information given above allows, for the following accounting items.

(1) Share capital
(2) Directors' remuneration (60 mins)

(c) The directors of the company are unclear as to the nature of goodwill. They have asked you to define it (4 mins)

WOODPECKER LIMITED
EXTENDED TRIAL BALANCE AS AT 31 MARCH 20X4

	Ledger balances DR £'000	Ledger balances CR £'000	Adjustments DR £'000	Adjustments CR £'000	Profit & Loss Account DR £'000	Profit & Loss Account CR £'000	Balance Sheet Balances DR £'000	Balance Sheet Balances CR £'000
Salaries and wages	1,468				1,468			
Salesmen's commission	102		4		106			
Motor expenses	72		6		78			
Sales		8,086				8,086		
Buildings (acc dep)		117		21				138
Fixtures and fittings (acc dep)		176		65				241
Motor vehicles (acc dep)		219		189				408
Office equipment (acc dep)		51		37				88
Investment revaluation reserve		150						150
Directors' pension contributions	15				15			
Advertising	67			11	56			
Stock	731		937	937	731	937	937	
Trade debtors	840						840	
Provision for doubtful debts		20		17				37
Goodwill	20						20	
Purchases	5,035				5,035			
Land and buildings (cost)	1,267						1,267	
Fixtures and fittings (cost)	632						632	
Motor vehicles (cost)	745						745	
Office equipment (cost)	194						194	
Investment property	800						800	
Depreciation (motor vehicles)			189		189			
Depreciation (fixtures and fittings)			65		65			
Depreciation (office equipment)			37		37			
Depreciation (buildings)			21		21			
Ordinary share capital		1,000						1,000
10% Preference share capital		300						300
Directors' fees	7				7			
Share premium		250						250
Light and heat	19		7		26			
Interim dividend	15				15			
Increase in provision for doubtful debt			17		17			
General expenses	227		28	21	234			
Insurance	45			7	38			
Profit and loss account		778						778
Accruals				45				45
Prepayments			39				39	
Cash in hand	3						3	
Cash at bank		139						139
Trade creditors		568						568
8% Debentures		450						450
Profit					885			885
	12,304	12,304	1,350	1,350	9,023	9,023	5,477	5,477

27   TINY TOYS (80 mins)

You have just begun work as the assistant to the Financial Director of Tiny Toys Ltd, a company which buys and sells toys. Your predecessor prepared an extended trial balance for the year ending 31 December 20X3 prior to leaving. This includes the normal year-end adjustments. The Financial Director has asked you to review the trial balance in the light of some further information which may be relevant to the accounts. She has asked you to make any adjustments necessary before they are published.

The extended trial balance of Tiny Toys Ltd is set out on page 36.

The following information is provided.

(a)   An audit fee of £950 needs to be provided for.

(b)   The amount representing share capital and reserves in the extended trial balance consists of 100,000 25p shares. The first issue of 50,000 shares was at par, a subsequent issue of 50,000 shares being at a premium of 30p and this balance remains in its entirety in the share premium account. The remainder consists of the brought forward balance on the profit and loss reserve.

(c)   A decision has been made to use half of the share premium account to make a bonus issue of ordinary 25p shares. No entries have been made in the extended trial balance to reflect this issue.

(d)   The amounts for rates and the depreciation of buildings should be split 50:50 between administrative and distribution cost classifications.

(e)   Included in the salaries are directors' emoluments of £45,000 of which £25,000 should be classed as administrative costs, the remainder being distribution costs. Also included in the salaries figure is £5,000 of the salesmen's commission. The remainder of the salaries and wages should be split 60% administration and 40% distribution costs.

(f)   Eighty per cent of the depreciation charge for vehicles should be classified as a distribution cost, the remainder being an administrative cost. The office equipment depreciation should be classed as an administrative expense.

(g)   Of the light and heat costs, £1,000 should be classed as administrative costs, the remainder being distribution.

(h)   £6,000 of the total motor expense are distribution costs, the remainder being administrative.

(i)   General expenses should be classed as administrative expenditure.

(j)   A building costing £35,000, NBV £32,500 was sold for £37,500. The correct entries have been made in the buildings cost and depreciation accounts, as well as the bank account, but the profit figure does not appear to have been entered in the ETB profit and loss account.

(k)   On 1 December 20X3 there was an issue of 10,000 £1 nominal 12% debentures at par. The issue has been correctly accounted for but no interest has been accrued.

(l)   The coding on the suspense account entry for £150 indicates it is an amount owing for motor expenses.

(m) There is no tax charge for the year.

TINY TOYS LIMITED
EXTENDED TRIAL BALANCE AS AT 31 DECEMBER 20X3

Folio Description	Ledger balances DR £	Ledger balances CR £	Adjustments DR £	Adjustments CR £	Profit & Loss Account DR £	Profit & Loss Account CR £	Balance Sheet Balances DR £	Balance Sheet Balances CR £
Sales		183,500				183,500		
Purchases	114,300				114,300			
Carriage outwards	3,100				3,100			
Motor expenses	6,600		150		6,750			
Rates	3,900			330	3,750			
Advertising	2,200				2,200			
Salaries and wages	75,000				75,000			
Debtors	38,900						38,900	
Creditors		17,000						17,000
Cash in hand	500						500	
Cash at bank	4,000						4,000	
Stock 01.07.X3	12,800		12,900	12,900	12,800	12,900	12,900	
Vehicles: cost	20,000						20,000	
Vehicles: depreciation		7,500		2,500				10,000
Office equipment: cost	4,000						4,000	
Office equipment: depreciation		1,000		500				1,500
Buildings: cost	40,000						40,000	
Buildings: depreciation		8,000		4,000				12,000
General expenses	500				500			
Provision for doubtful debts		1,800		200				2,000
Increase in prov for doubtful debts			200		200			
Bad debt	1,000				1,000			
Depreciation: vehicles			2,500		2,500			
Depreciation: office equipment			500		500			
Depreciation: buildings			4,000		4,000			
Light and heat	1,700		150		1,850			
Loss						31,870	31,870	
Prepayment (rates)			330				330	
Accrual (light and heat)				150				150
Debentures		10,000						10,000
Share capital and reserves		94,700						94,700
Suspense		5,000		150				5,150
	328,500	328,500	20,730	20,730	228,270	228,270	152,500	152,500

Tasks

(a) Make any adjustments you feel necessary to the balances in the extended trial balance as a result of the matters set out in the information above. Set out your adjustments in the form of journal entries. (Ignore the effect of any adjustments on taxation.) (16 mins)

(b) Draft a profit and loss account for the year ended 31 December 20X3 and a balance sheet as at that date in a form suitable for publication using Format 1 in accordance with the Companies Act as supplemented by FRS 3 *Reporting financial performance*. (You are *not* required to prepare a statement of total recognised gains and losses or the reconciliation of movements in shareholders' funds required under FRS 3.) You should assume that all the information relates to continuing operations. (40 mins)

(c) You have been asked to comment briefly on the following.

    (i)   The constituents of the working capital of Tiny Toys Ltd   (6 mins)
    (ii)   The profitability of Tiny Toys Ltd   (3 mins)
    (iii) The difference between cash flow and profitability   (3 mins)

(d) The Companies Act and SSAP 2 require the disclosure of accounting policies in the notes to the accounts. Explain why this is useful to users of accounts, illustrating your answer with reference to:

    (i)   Depreciation
    (ii)   Research and development
    (iii) Stock   (12 mins)

28   FRANCO (105 mins)   6/95

You are employed by a firm of certified accountants and have been asked to prepare the financial statements of Franco Ltd (a company which distributes confectionery) for the year ending 31 March 20X5. A bookkeeper at the company has prepared an extended trial balance for the year ending 31 March 20X5; this includes the normal year-end adjustments. You have been asked to review the trial balance in the light of some further information which may be relevant to the accounts and to make any adjustments necessary before they are published.

The extended trial balance of Franco Ltd is set out on page 38.

The following further information is provided.

(a) The corporation tax charge for the year has been agreed at £110,000.

(b) Motor expenses of £10,000 and wages of £2,000 have been wrongly included in the general expenses figure in the trial balance. Of the remaining general expenses, £100,000 should be classified as administrative, the balance being distribution expenses.

(c) The amount representing share capital and reserves in the extended trial balance consists of 400,000 50p ordinary shares and 50,000 £1 (8%) preference shares. The directors have just declared the final dividend for the ordinary shares and this has not yet been entered into the accounts. The preference dividend also needs to be provided for. The total (ordinary and preference) dividend for the year amounts to £72,000.

(d) Interest due on the long-term loan for the year needs to be provided for; it is charged at 10% per annum.

(e) An audit fee of £9,000 needs to be provided for.

FRANCO LIMITED
EXTENDED TRIAL BALANCE AS AT 31 MARCH 20X5

Folio	Description	Ledger balances DR £'000	Ledger balances CR £'000	Adjustments DR £'000	Adjustments CR £'000	Profit & Loss Account DR £'000	Profit & Loss Account CR £'000	Balance Sheet Balances DR £'000	Balance Sheet Balances CR £'000
	Turnover		2,470				2,470		
	Purchases	1,000				1,000			
	Salaries and wages	400				400			
	Motor expenses	27				27			
	Rates	25			5	20			
	Light and heat	32		4		36			
	Carriage inwards	14				14			
	Advertising	95				95			
	Stock	215		225	225	215	225	225	
	Trade debtors	450						450	
	Provision for doubtful debts		6		3				9
	Increase in prov for doubtful debts			3		3			
	Cash in hand	1						1	
	Cash at bank	6						6	
	Trade creditors		170						170
	Land (cost)	375						375	
	Buildings (cost)	200						200	
	Fixtures and fittings (cost)	35						35	
	Motor vehicles (cost)	94						94	
	Office equipment (cost)	20						20	
	Buildings (acc dep)		20		4				24
	Fixtures and fittings (acc dep)		18		5				23
	Motor vehicles (acc dep)		54		10				64
	Office equipment (acc dep)		4		1				5
	Depreciation - buildings			4		4			
	Depreciation - fixtures and fittings			5		5			
	Depreciation - motor vehicles			10		10			
	Depreciation - office equipment			1		1			
	Returns inwards	10				10			
	Interim dividend	30				30			
	Returns outwards		5				5		
	General expenses	135				135			
	Insurance	13			1	12			
	Profit and loss account		160						160
	Accruals				4				4
	Prepayment			6				6	
	Share capital - ordinary shares		200						200
	Share capital - preference shares		50						50
	Long term loan		20						20
	Profit					683			683
		3,177	3,177	258	258	2,700	2,700	1,412	1,412

(f) Included in the total salaries figure is £98,000 of directors' emoluments. £68,000 of directors' emoluments should be classed as administrative expenses, the remainder being distribution. £104,000 of salaries and wages (excluding directors' emoluments) should be classed as administrative expenses, the remainder being distribution expenses.

(g) Rates and light and heat should be split equally between administration and distribution expenses.

(h) £27,000 of motor expenses are to be classed as distribution, the remainder as administration expenses.

(i) The depreciation charges should be classed as:

	Administration £	Distribution £
Buildings	3,000	1,000
Fixtures and fittings	4,000	1,000
Motor vehicles	2,000	8,000
Office	1,000	-

(j) The insurance payment should be split in the ratio of 75/25 between administration and distribution expenses respectively.

Tasks

(a) Make any adjustments you feel necessary to the balances in the extended trial balance as a result of the matters set out in the further information on page 186. Set out your adjustments in the form of journal entries. (Ignore the effect of any adjustments on the tax charge for the year.

(b) Draft a profit and loss account for the year ended 31 March 20X5 and a balance sheet as at that date in a form suitable for publication using Format 1 in accordance with the Companies Act as supplemented by FRS 3 *Reporting financial performance*. (You are *not* required to prepare a statement of total recognised gains and losses or the reconciliation of movements in shareholders' funds required under FRS 3.)

(c) You have been asked by the directors of the company to prepare a short report covering the following.

  (i)   Stock is valued at the lower of cost and net realisable value in the accounts in accordance with SSAP 9. The directors would like you to explain how cost and net realisable value are derived.

  (ii) The directors have heard of the filing exemptions available to small companies, and they would like you to explain what these exemptions are.

  Write a report which covers the required points.

(d) The Directors of Franco Ltd have drawn your attention to three matters and requested your advice on how these should be treated.

  (i)   An issue of shares was made on 10 April 20X5. Fifty thousand 50p ordinary shares were issued at a premium of 25p.

  (ii) A debtor owing £30,000 to Franco Ltd on 31 March 20X5 went into liquidation on 3 April 20X5. The £30,000 is still unpaid and it is unclear whether any monies will be received.

  (iii) The company is awaiting the outcome of a legal suit; an independent lawyer has assessed that it is probable that the company will gain £25,000 from it.

Write a memo to the directors of Franco Ltd outlining the required treatment for *each* of the three events.

(e) Financial statements should be prepared on the basis of conditions which exist at the balance sheet date. The term 'window dressing' is used to describe a situation where transactions have been undertaken just before the balance sheet date and will be reversed after that date, simply to improve the appearance of the position of the company at the year end.

   (i)   Give two examples of how window dressing may be used to improve the cash balance in the balance sheet.

   (ii) Explain how SSAP 17 *Post balance sheet events* requires window dressing to be dealt with.

29   LAWNDERER (90 mins)   12/95

You have been asked to assist the directors of Lawnderer Ltd, a company that markets and distributes lawnmowers and other garden machinery, in the preparation of the financial statements for the year ended 30 September 20X5. The company employs a bookkeeper who is competent in some areas of financial accounting but has gaps in his knowledge which you are required to fill. He has already prepared the extended trial balance which is set out on page 41.

The following further information is provided by the bookkeeper.

(a) The company disposed of motor vehicles during the year. The cost of the vehicles of £491,000 and the accumulated depreciation of £368,000 are still included in the figures in the trial balance. The sale proceeds of £187,000 were credited to the sales account.

(b) Salesmen's commission of £52,000 relating to sales in the year has not been paid or charged as an expense in the figures in the trial balance.

(c) Interest on the 9% debentures has been included in the trial balance only for the first six months of the year.

(d) The tax charge for the year has been calculated at £843,000.

(e) A final dividend of 5 pence per share has yet to be provided for. The authorised and issued share capital of the company consists of shares with a nominal value of 25p.

(f) Goodwill is being written off on a straight-line basis over a period of 10 years, but no amortisation has yet been charged in the trial balance.

(g) The doubtful debts provision in the trial balance has not yet been adjusted for this year. The total doubtful debts provision required has been calculated at £115,000.

The directors of the company have also had a meeting with you regarding the possible treatment of certain future expenditure in the financial statements of the company. They have told you that the company has been approached by an inventor who has an idea to develop a revolutionary new lawnmower. The project looks technically feasible and preliminary marketing studies suggest a significant market for the product. Cost and revenue projections suggest that future profits should adequately cover the cost of development and have a beneficial effect on the future profitability of the company. The only problem the directors foresee is how to finance the operation to completion given the high level of borrowing already in the company. Their other concern is the effect that the expenditure on developing the new product will have on future profits, given that it will take some time between commencing the project and commercial production.

LAWNDERER LIMITED: EXTENDED TRIAL BALANCE 30 SEPTEMBER 20X5

Folio	Description	Trial balance Debit £'000	Trial balance Credit £'000	Adjustments Debit £'000	Adjustments Credit £'000	Profit and loss account Debit £'000	Profit and loss account Credit £'000	Balance sheet Debit £'000	Balance sheet Credit £'000
	Depreciation: Land and buildings			18		18			
	Fixtures and fittings			72		72			
	Motor vehicles			298		298			
	Office equipment			24		24			
	Goodwill	360						360	
	Accruals				102				102
	Dividends	120				120			
	Interest on debentures	153				153			
	Net sales		22,129				22,129		
	Trade debtors	2,603						2,603	
	Prepayments			43				43	
	Bank overdraft		362						362
	Cash in hand	3						3	
	Purchases	14,112				14,112			
	Stock 1.10.X4	3,625				3,625			
	Stock 30.9.X5			4,572	4,572		4,572	4,572	
	Profit and loss account 1.10.X4	134						134	
	Provision for doubtful debts		78						78
	Trade creditors		2,967						2,967
	Distribution costs	4,028		37	25	4,040			
	9% Debentures		3,400						3,400
	Administration expenses	1,736		65	18	1,783			
	Accumulated depreciation: Land and buildings		83		18				101
	Fixtures and fittings		214		72				286
	Motor vehicles		644		298				942
	Office equipment		83		24				107
	Land and buildings (cost)	1,875						1,875	
	Fixtures and fittings (cost)	576						576	
	Motor vehicles (cost)	1,691						1,691	
	Office equipment (cost)	244						244	
	Called up share capital		1,000						1,000
	Share premium		300						300
	Profit					2,456			2,456
		31,260	31,260	5,129	5,129	26,701	26,701	12,101	12,101

The directors have also asked you, at the same meeting, about the contents of the directors' report.

Tasks

(a) (i) Make any adjustments you feel to be necessary to the balances in the extended trial balance as a result of the matters set out in the further information given by the bookkeeper above. Set out your adjustments in the form of journal entries (narratives are not required).

(ii) Calculate the new retained profit which would result from these adjustments being made.

(Ignore any effect of these adjustments on the tax charge for the year as given above.)

(b) Draft a balance sheet for the year ended 30 September 20X5, in a form suitable for publication, using Format 1 in accordance with the Companies Act 1985.

(c) Answer the following questions of the directors arising out of the further information given to you by them.

(i) How would the costs of developing the new lawnmower be reflected in the future results of the company?

(ii) What is 'gearing'? Would Lawnderer Ltd be considered to be a highly geared company and, if so, how might this affect the decision of a potential lender to lend money to the company?

(d) The directors are also aware that a directors' report has to be produced with the financial statements. State *four* things that must appear in the directors' report, with a brief explanation of their nature.

30 DOWANGO (54 mins)   6/96

You have been assigned to assist in the preparation of the financial statements of Dowango Ltd for the year ended 31 March 20X6. The company is a cash and carry operation that trades from a large warehouse on an industrial estate. You have been provided with the extended trial balance of Dowango Ltd on 31 March 20X6 which is set out on page 43.

You have been given the following further information.

(a) The authorised and issued share capital of the business consists of ordinary shares with a nominal value of £1.

(b) The company has paid an interim dividend of 4p per share during the year but has not provided for the final dividend of 6p per share.

(c) Depreciation has been calculated on all of the fixed assets of the business and has already been entered on a monthly basis into the distribution expenses and administration costs ledger balances as shown on the extended trial balance.

(d) The tax charge for the year has been calculated as £211,000.

(e) Interest on the long-term loan has been paid for six months of the year. No adjustment has been made for the interest due for the final six months of the year. Interest is charged on the loan at a rate of 10% per annum.

(f) An advertising campaign was undertaken during the year at a cost of £19,000. No invoices have yet been received for this campaign and no adjustment for this expense has been made in the extended trial balance.

DOWANGO LIMITED: EXTENDED TRIAL BALANCE AS AT 31 MARCH 20X6

Description	Trial balance		Adjustments		Profit and loss a/c		Balance sheet	
	Debit £'000	*Credit* £'000	*Debit* £'000	*Credit* £'000	*Debit* £'000	*Credit* £'000	*Debit* £'000	*Credit* £'000
Land (cost)	431						431	
Buildings (cost)	512						512	
Fixtures & fittings (cost)	389						389	
Motor vehicles (cost)	341						341	
Office equipment - (cost)	105						105	
Buildings - (accumulated depreciation)		184						184
Fixtures & fittings - (accumulated depreciation)		181						181
Motor vehicles - (accumulated depreciation)		204						204
Office equipment - (accumulated depreciation)		56						56
Stock	298		365	365	298	365	365	
Investments	64						64	
Debtors	619						619	
Provision for doubtful debts		27						27
Prepayments			21				21	
Cash in hand	3						3	
Cash at bank		157						157
Creditors		331						331
Accruals				41				41
Sales		5,391				5,391		
Purchases	2,988				2,988			
Returns inwards	39				39			
Returns outwards		31				31		
Carriage inwards	20				20			
Distribution expenses	1,092		23	11	1,104			
Administrative costs	701		18	10	709			
Interest charges	15				15			
Interim dividend	20				20			
Share capital		500						500
Profit and loss account		275						275
Long term loan		300						300
Profit					594			594
	7,637	7,637	427	427	5,787	5,787	2,850	2,850

(g) The investments consist of shares in a retail company that were purchased with a view to resale at a profit. Dowango Ltd own 2% of the share capital of the company. At the end of the year a valuation of the shares was obtained with a view to selling the shares in the forthcoming year. The shares were valued at £56,000.

Tasks

(a) Make any adjustments you feel to be necessary to the balances in the extended trial balance as a result of the matters set out in the further information above. Set out your adjustments in the form of journal entries. Narratives are not required. (Ignore any effect of these adjustments on the tax charge for the year as given above.)

(b) Draft a profit and loss account for the year ended 31 March 20X6 and a balance sheet as at that date using Format 1 in accordance with the Companies Act 1985 as supplemented by FRS 3 *Reporting financial performance*.

(Your are *not* required to prepare a statement of total recognised gains and losses or the reconciliation of movements in shareholders' funds required under FRS 3.)

(c) The directors of Dowango Ltd have asked to have a meeting with you. They are intending to ask the bank for a further long-term loan to enable them to purchase a company which has retail outlets. The directors have identified two possible companies to take over and they intend to purchase the whole of the share capital of one of the two targeted companies. The directors have obtained the latest financial statements of the two companies in summary form, and have also sent you a letter with some questions that they would like you to answer. The financial statements and the letter are set out below and on page 45.

SUMMARY PROFIT AND LOSS ACCOUNTS

	Company A £'000	Company B £'000
Turnover	800	2,100
Cost of sales	440	1,050
Gross profit	360	1,050
Expenses	160	630
Net profit before interest and tax	200	420

SUMMARY BALANCE SHEETS

	Company A £'000	Company B £'000
Fixed assets	620	1,640
Net current assets	380	1,160
Long-term loan	(400)	(1,100)
	600	1,700
Share capital and reserves	600	1,700

DOWANGO LTD

Dear AAT student

In preparation for discussions about a possible loan to Dowango Ltd, the bank has asked to see the latest financial statements of Dowango Ltd. We wish to ensure that the financial statements show the company in the best light. In particular, we wish to ensure that the assets of the business are shown at their proper value. We would like to discuss with you the following issues.

(a) The fixed assets of our company are undervalued. We have received a professional valuation of the land and buildings which shows that they are worth more than is stated in our financial statements. The land has a current market value of £641,000 and the buildings are valued at £558,000.

(b) The investments are recorded in our trial balance at cost. We realise that the market value of the investments is less than the cost, but since we have not yet sold it, we have not made a loss on it and so we should continue to show it at cost.

(c) Stocks are recorded in our balance sheet at cost. Most of our stock is worth more than this as we could sell it for more than we paid for it. Only a few items would sell for less than we paid for them. We have worked out the real value of our stock as follows.

	Cost	Sales prices
	£,000	£,000
Undervalued items	340	460
Overvalued items	25	15
Total	365	475

We have set out a number of questions we would like answered at our meeting in an appendix to this letter. We would also like you to advise us at that meeting on the profitability and return on capital of the two companies targeted for takeover (whose financial statements we have already sent to you) and on the reporting implications if we purchase one of the companies.

Yours sincerely

The directors

(i) The questions from the appendix to the directors' letter are shown below. Write a memo to the directors answering these questions, which relate to the financial statements of Dowango Ltd. Explain your answers, where relevant, by reference to company law, accounting concepts and applicable accounting standards.

(1) Can we show the land and buildings at valuation rather than cost?

(2) If we did so, how would the valuation of land and buildings be reflected in the financial statements?

(3) Would revaluing the land and buildings have any effect upon the gearing ratio of the company and would this assist us in our attempt to get a loan from the bank?

(4) What effect would a revaluation have upon the future results of the company?

(ii) Can we continue to show the investments at cost?

(iii) What is the best value for stock that we can show in our balance sheet in the light of the information we have given you about sales price?

(d) Advise the directors as to which of the two companies targeted for takeover is the more profitable and which one provides the higher return on capital. Your answer should include calculation of the following ratios.

(i) Return on capital employed
(ii) Net profit margin
(iii) Asset turnover

You should also calculate and comment on at least one further ratio of your choice, for which you have sufficient information, which would be relevant to determining which of the companies is more profitable or provides the greater return on capital.

(e) Advise the directors as to whether Dowango Ltd would have any further reporting requirements in the future as a result of the purchase of shares in one of the companies targeted for takeover.

---

31   SPIRAES (40 mins)   **12/96**

You have been assigned to assist in the preparation of the financial statements of Spiraes Ltd for the year ended 30 November 20X6. The company is a trading company operating from freehold premises in a large industrial city. You have been provided with the extended trial balance of Spiraes Ltd on 30 November 20X6, which is set out on page 47.

You have been given the following further information.

(a) The share capital of the business consists of ordinary shares with a nominal value of 25p.

(b) The company has paid no interim dividend this year but is proposing to provide a final dividend of 2 pence per share for the year.

(c) Depreciation has been calculated on all of the fixed assets of the business and has already been entered on a monthly basis into the distribution expenses and administration expenses ledger balances as shown on the extended trial balance.

(d) The tax charge for the year has been calculated as £1,356,000.

(e) Interest on the 9% debentures has been paid for the first six months of the year only. No adjustment has been made for the interest due for the final six months of the year.

(f) The land has been valued at market value at the end of the year by a professional valuer at £4,290,000. It is proposed that the valuation be incorporated into the financial statements of the company as at 30 November 20X6.

(g) The fixed asset investment consists of shares in a publicly quoted company and is shown in the extended trial balance at cost. The investment represents 7% of the total issued ordinary share capital of the quoted company and was purchased with the intention of investing in the company on a long-term basis.

(h) Some items of stock which were included in the stock balance in the extended trial balance at a cost of £405,000 were sold after the year end for £355,000.

SPIRAES LIMITED

EXTENDED TRIAL BALANCE 30 NOVEMBER 20X6

	Trial balance		Adjustments		Profit and loss account		Balance sheet	
	Debit £'000	Credit £'000	Debit £'000	Credit £'000	Debit £'000	Credit £'000	Debit £'000	Credit £'000
Trade creditors		2,653						2,653
Accruals				63				63
Cash at bank	375						375	
Interest charges	189				189			
Buildings - accumulated depreciation		810						810
Office equipment - accumulated depreciation		319						319
Motor vehicles - accumulated depreciation		1,912						1,912
Fixtures and fittings - accumulated depreciation		820						820
Sales		18,742				18,742		
Trade debtors	3,727						3,727	
Provision for doubtful debts		68						68
Dividends received		52				52		
Fixed asset investment	866						866	
Profit and loss account		6,192						6,192
9% debentures		4,200						4,200
Prepayments			31				31	
Land - cost	3,570						3,570	
Buildings - cost	2,933						2,933	
Office equipment - cost	882						882	
Motor vehicles - cost	3,485						3,485	
Fixtures and fittings - cost	2,071						2,071	
Purchases	10,776				10,776			
Administrative expenses	1,805		27	12	1,820			
Stock	3,871		4,153	4,153	3,871	4,153	4,153	
Returns inwards	595				595			
Returns outwards		314				314		
Ordinary share capital		1,000						1,000
Share premium		560						560
Distribution costs	2,497		36	19	2,514			
Profit					3,496			3,496
	37,642	37,642	4,247	4,247	23,261	23,261	22,093	22,093

Tasks

(a) Make any additional adjustments you feel to be necessary to the balances in the extended trial balance as a result of the matters set out in the further information above. Set out your adjustments in the form of journal entries.

Note

(1) Narratives are not required.

(2) Ignore any effect of these adjustments on the tax charge for the year as given above.

(b) Justify your treatment of items (f) and (h) in the further information above. Refer in your answer, where relevant, to company law, accounting concepts and applicable accounting standards.

(c) Draft a profit and loss account for the year ended 30 November 20X6 using Format 1 in accordance with the Companies Act 1985 as supplemented by FRS 3 *Reporting financial performance*.

Note

You are not required to prepare a balance sheet or the reconciliation of movements in shareholders' funds required under FRS 3.

(d) Prepare a statement of total recognised gains and losses for the year ended 30 November 20X6 for Spiraes Ltd as required by FRS 3.

32   PRIMAVERA FASHIONS (50 mins)   6/97

You have been assigned to assist in the preparation of the financial statements of Primavera Fashions Ltd for the year ended 31 March 20X7. The company is a trading company which distributes fashion clothing. It has one subsidiary undertaking and one associated company.

Primavera Fashions Ltd recently engaged a financial accountant to manage a team of book-keepers. The book-keepers produced a correct extended trial balance of the company and gave it to the accountant so that he could draft the year end financial statements.

The book-keeping staff have reported that he appeared to have some difficulty with the task and, after several days, apparently gave up the task and has not been seen since. He left behind him a balance sheet and some pages of workings which appear to contain a number of errors.

There is to be a meeting of the Board next week at which the financial statements will be approved. You have been brought in to assist in the production of a corrected balance sheet and to advise the directors on matters concerning the year end accounts. The uncorrected balance sheet, the workings left by the financial accountant and the correct extended trial balance of Primavera Fashions Ltd on 31 March 20X7 are set out on the following pages.

PRIMAVERA FASHIONS LIMITED
BALANCE SHEET AS AT 31 MARCH 20X7

	£'000	£'000
Fixed assets		
Intangible assets		128
Tangible assets		3,948
Investments		2,924
		7,000
Current assets		
Stocks	1,097	
Debtors	924	
Cash at bank and in hand	152	
	2,173	
Creditors: amounts falling due within one year	2,486	
Net current assets (liabilities)		(313)
Total assets less current liabilities		6,687
Creditors: amounts falling due after more than one year		800
		5,887
Capital and reserves		
Called up share capital		1,000
Revaluation reserve		550
Profit and loss account		4,051
		5,601

Workings

1   *Fixed assets*

	Cost	Acc. Depn.	NBV
	£'000	£'000	£'000
Land	525		525
Buildings	1,000	50	950
Fixtures & fittings	1,170	117	1,053
Motor vehicles	1,520	380	1,140
Office equipment	350	70	280
	4,565	617	3,948

2   *Debtors*

	£'000	£'000
Trade debtors	857	
Plus accruals	104	
		961
Less prepayments		(37)
		924

3   *Creditors: amounts falling due within one year*

	£'000
Trade creditors	483
Corporation tax payable	382
Dividends payable	60
Provision for doubtful debts	61
10% Debentures	1,500
	2,486

4   *Creditors: amounts falling due after more than one year*

	£'000
Share premium	800

5   *Profit and loss account*

	£'000
At 1/4/X6	2,819
Retained profit for the year	1,232
At 31/3/X7	4,051

PRIMAVERA FASHIONS LTD
EXTENDED TRIAL BALANCE 31 MARCH 20X7

DESCRIPTION	TRIAL BALANCE Debit £'000	TRIAL BALANCE Credit £'000	ADJUSTMENTS Debit £'000	ADJUSTMENTS Credit £'000	PROFIT AND LOSS Debit £'000	PROFIT AND LOSS Credit £'000	BALANCE SHEET Debit £'000	BALANCE SHEET Credit £'000
Profit and loss account		2,819						2,819
Land - cost	525						525	
Buildings - cost	1,000						1,000	
Fixtures & fittings - cost	1,170						1,170	
Motor vehicles - cost	1,520						1,520	
Office equipment	350						350	
Sales		12,604				12,604		
Buildings - accumulated depreciation		170		50				220
Fixtures & fittings - accumulated depreciation		229		117				346
Motor vehicles - accumulated depreciation		203		380				583
Office equipment - accumulated depreciation		73		70				143
Stock	1,097		1,178	1,178	1,097	1,178	1,178	
Interest charges	153				153			
Goodwill	128						128	
Trade debtors	857						857	
Purchases	7,604				7,604			
Interim dividend	160				160			
Investments	2,924						2,924	
Cash at bank	152						152	
Distribution costs	1,444		68	17	1,495			
Administrative expenses	1,441		36	20	1,457			
Depreciation - buildings			50		50			
Depreciation - fixtures and fittings			117		117			
Depreciation - motor vehicles			380		380			
Depreciation - office equipment			70		70			
Share capital		1,000						1,000
Provision for doubtful debts		61						61
Trade creditors		483						483
Accruals		23		104				104
Dividends from subsidiary undertaking						23		
Prepayments			37				37	
Dividends from associated company		10				10		
10% Debentures		1,500						1,500
Share premium		800						800
Revaluation reserve		550						550
Profit					1,232			1,232
	20,525	20,525	1,936	1,936	13,815	13,815	9,841	9,841

You have also received the following additional information to assist you in your task.

(a) The share capital consists of ordinary shares with a nominal value of 25 pence. The company has paid an interim dividend during the year and the directors have recommended a final dividend of 6 pence per share, which has not been provided for in the extended trial balance.

(b) The tax charge for the year has been estimated at £382,000.

(c) The investments shown on the extended trial balance relate to long-term investment in the shares of one subsidiary undertaking and one associated company.

Tasks

(a) Redraft the company balance sheet for Primavera Fashions Ltd as at 31 March 20X7. Make any changes that you feel to be necessary to the balance sheet and workings provided by the financial accountant using the information contained in the extended trial balance for the year ended 31 March 20X7.

Note. You are *not* required to produce a profit and loss account.

The directors of Primavera Fashions Ltd have asked you to prepare some answers to certain questions they have relating to the year end financial statements that are due to be considered at next week's meeting of the Board.

The directors are uncertain as to how the balance on the share premium account arose and how it can be used.

The directors have just learned that one of their trade debtors has gone into liquidation owing them £24,000. The liquidator has informed them that it is likely that there will be no assets available to pay off creditors and they wonder whether this will have any effect on the financial statements for the year ended 31 March 20X7.

The directors are also uncertain as to the accounting treatment of their investment in shares of an associated company, Spring Ltd. Primavera Fashions Ltd purchased a 35% interest in the company for £400,000 in 20X5 when the total net assets of the company amounted to £800,000. (There was no goodwill shown in the associated company's own balance sheet.) Since acquisition Spring Ltd has made profits amounting to £200,000 and, as at 31 March 20X7, the total net assets of the company amounted to £1,000,000.

(b) Reply to the following questions from the directors. Where appropriate, justify your answers by reference to company law, accounting concepts and applicable accounting standards.

(i) (1) How did the balance on the share premium arise?
(2) Can it be used to pay dividends to the shareholders?
(3) Give one use of the share premium account.

(ii) Will the fact that the debtor went into liquidation after the end of the financial year have any impact upon the financial statements for the year ended 31 March 20X7?

(iii) (1) At what amount will the investment in Spring Ltd be shown in the group balance sheet as at 31 March 20X7?

(2) Show how the total investment in Spring Ltd will be analysed in the notes to the group financial statements.

33   DESKCOVER (90 mins)   **Specimen**

You have been assigned to assist in the preparation of the financial statements of Deskcover Ltd for the year ended 31 December 20X7. The company is a wholesale distributor of office equipment. You have been provided with the extended trial balance of Deskcover Ltd as at 31 December 20X7 which is set out on page 53.

You have been given the following further information

(a)   The authorised share capital of the business, all of which has been issued, consists of ordinary shares with a nominal value of £1.

(b)   Depreciation has been calculated on all of the fixed assets of the business and has already been entered on a monthly basis into the distribution expenses and administration costs ledger balances as shown on the extended trial balance.

(c)   The corporation tax charge for the year has been calculated as £726,000.

(d)   The company has paid an interim dividend of 6p per share during the year but has not provided for the proposed final dividend of 8p per share.

(e)   Interest on the 8% debentures has been paid for the first six months of the year only.

Tasks

(a)   Taking into account the further information provided, draft a profit and loss account for the year ended 31 December 20X7 and a balance sheet as at that date.

   Notes

   1   You must show any *workings* relevant to understanding your calculation of figures appearing in the financial statements.

   2   You are *not* required to produce journal entries for any necessary adjustments to the figures in the extended trial balance.

   3   Ignore any effect of these adjustments on the tax charge for the year as given above.

(b)   Following your preparation of the balance sheet and profit and loss account of Deskcover Ltd, you have had a meeting with the directors at which certain other matters were raised. These are set out below.

   (i)   One of the debtors of Deskcover Ltd has been having cashflow problems. The balance at the end of the year was £186,000. Against this there was a specific provision of £93,000. After the year end, the directors received a letter from the liquidators of the debtor stating that the business had gone into liquidation on 14 January 20X8. The liquidators have stated that there will be no assets available to meet any of the debts of the unsecured creditors.

   (ii) The investment of £4,010,000 shown in the extended trial balance of Deskcover Ltd represents the cost of acquiring shares in a subsidiary undertaking, Underdesk Ltd. Deskcover Ltd acquired 75% of the ordinary share capital of Underdesk Ltd on 31 December 20X7. The directors have obtained a balance sheet and a profit and loss account of the company for the last two years that have been prepared for internal purposes. They have not yet received the cashflow statement, which they would like to inspect. Underdesk Ltd's year end is also 31 December. The net assets of Underdesk Ltd are shown in the balance sheet at their fair values except for the fixed assets, which have a fair value at 31 December 20X7 of £5,761,000.

DESKCOVER LIMITED – EXTENDED TRIAL BALANCE AS OF 31 DECEMBER 20X7

	Trial balance		Adjustments		Profit and loss		Balance sheet	
	Debit £'000	Credit £'000	Debit £'000	Credit £'000	Debit £'000	Credit £'000	Debit £'000	Credit £'000
Cash at bank	316						316	
8% debentures		3,400						3,400
Trade debtors	3,386						3,386	
Provision for doubtful debts		125		44				169
Sales		20,469				20,469		
Purchases	12,025				12,025			
Land - cost	1,602						1,602	
Buildings - cost	2,137						2,137	
Fixtures & fittings - cost	1,399						1,399	
Motor vehicles - cost	1,786						1,786	
Office equipment - cost	402						402	
Returns inwards	152				152			
Stock	4,502		5,244	5,244	4,502	5,244	5,244	
Accruals				118				118
Prepayments			56				56	
Returns outwards		109				109		
Buildings - acc dep'n		413		214				627
Fixtures & fittings - acc dep'n		404		350				754
Motor vehicles - acc dep'n		486		417				903
Office equipment - acc dep'n		45		68				113
Interim dividend	240				240			
Trade creditors		2,035						2,035
Interest	136				136			
Distribution costs	3,214		542		3,756			
Admin expenses	2,368		613		2,981			
Investment	4,010						4,010	
Share capital		4,000						4,000
P&L account		4,389						4,389
Share premium		1,800						1,800
Profit					2,030			2,030
	37,675	37,675	6,455	6,455	25,822	25,822	20,338	20,338

UNDERDESK LIMITED
PROFIT AND LOSS ACCOUNT FOR THE YEAR ENDED 31 DECEMBER 20X7

	20X7 £'000	20X6 £'000
Turnover	5,490	4,573
Cost of sales	3,861	3,201
Gross profit	1,629	1,372
Depreciation	672	445
Other expenses	313	297
Profit on the sale of fixed assets	29	13
Operating profit for the year	673	643
Interest paid	156	47
Profit before tax	517	596
Taxation on profit	129	124
Profit after tax	388	472
Ordinary dividend	180	96
Retained profit	208	376

UNDERDESK LIMITED
BALANCE SHEET AS AT 31 DECEMBER 20X7

	20X7 £'000	20X7 £'000	20X6 £'000	20X6 £'000
Fixed assets		5,461		2,979
Current assets				
Stocks	607		543	
Debtors	481		426	
Cash	-		104	
	1,088		1,073	
Current liabilities				
Trade creditors	371		340	
Dividends payable	180		96	
Taxation	129		124	
Bank overdraft	89		-	
	769		560	
Net current assets		319		513
Long term loan		(1,700)		(520)
		4,080		2,972
Capital and reserves				
Called up share capital		1,400		800
Share premium		400		100
Profit and loss account		2,280		2,072
		4,080		2,972

Further information

- Fixed assets costing £187,000 with accumulated depreciation of £102,000 were sold in 20X7 for £114,000. There were no other disposals in the year.

- All sales and purchases were on credit. Other expenses were paid for in cash.

(i) State whether any adjustment needs to be made to the financial statements of Underdesk Ltd as a result of the liquidation of the debtor. Set out any adjustment required in the form of a journal entry and justify the accounting treatment by reference to applicable accounting standards.

Note. Narratives are not required for journal entries.

(ii) Provide a reconciliation between cash flows from operating activities and operating profit for the year ended 31 December 20X7 for Underdesk Ltd.

(iii) Prepare a cashflow statement for Underdesk Ltd for the year ended 31 December 20X7 in accordance with the requirements of FRS 1 (Revised).

(iv) Calculate the goodwill on consolidation that arose on acquisition of the shares in Underdesk Ltd on 31 December 20X7. Set out the possible accounting treatments of this goodwill in the group accounts of Deskcover Ltd, justifying your answer by reference to applicable accounting standards.

Note. You are *not* required to produce a consolidated balance sheet for the group.

34 SOLU (80 mins)   6/98

You have been asked to assist in the preparation of the financial statements of Solu Ltd for the year ended 31 March 20X8. The company runs a wholesale stationery and confectionery business for retailers. You have been provided with the extended trial balance of Solu Ltd for the year ended 31 March 20X8 which is set out on page 56.

You have also been given the following further information.

(a) The authorised and issued share capital of the business consists of ordinary shares with a nominal value of 25p.

(b) The company has paid an interim dividend of 2p per share. The company wishes to allow a total dividend of 6p per share for the year.

(c) The corporation tax charge for the year has been calculated as £75,000.

(d) Depreciation has been charged on all assets for the year and included in the trial balance figures for distribution costs and administrative expenses.

(e) The interest on the long-term loan is charged at 10% per annum. It is paid twice a year in arrears. The charge for the first six months of the year is included in the trial balance.

(f) The general provision for bad debts is to be adjusted to 2% of debtors.

(g) On 31 March 20X8 Solu Ltd bought 75% of the share capital of Edward Ltd for £200,000.

(h) The share capital and reserves of Edward Ltd at that date were as follows.

	£
Ordinary share capital (£1)	100,000
Share premium account	50,000
Profit and loss account	25,000

The fixed assets of Edward Ltd were included in the balance sheet at a net book value of £70,000 but a valuation on 31 March 20X8 valued them at £95,000.

Tasks

(a) Make the journal entries you feel to be necessary to the balances in the extended trial balance as a result of the matters set out in the further information above. Narratives are not required.

Notes

1 Ignore any effect of these adjustments on the tax charge for the year given above.

2 You must show any workings relevant to understanding your calculation of figures appearing in the financial statements.

SOLU LIMITED: EXTENDED TRIAL BALANCE 31 MARCH 20X8

Description	Trial balance		Adjustments		Profit and loss account		Balance sheet	
	Debit £'000	*Credit* £'000	*Debit* £'000	*Credit* £'000	*Debit* £'000	*Credit* £'000	*Debit* £'000	*Credit* £'000
Land and buildings - cost	268						268	
Fixtures and fittings - cost	100						100	
Motor vehicles - cost	120						120	
Office equipment - cost	90						90	
Land and buildings - accumulated depreciation		50						50
Fixtures and fittings - accumulated depreciation		35						35
Motor vehicles - accumulated depreciation		65						65
Office equipment - accumulated depreciation		45						45
Investment in Edward	200						200	
Sales		4,090				4,090		
Purchases	1,800				1,800			
Stock	300		320	320	300	320	320	
Debtors	500						500	
Provision for bad debts		1						1
Prepayments			15				15	
Bank overdraft		55						55
Creditors		459						459
Accruals				40				40
Carriage inwards	25				25			
Distribution costs	1,050		10	5	1,055			
Administrative expenses	970		30	10	990			
Interest charges	10				10			
Interim dividend	32				32			
Share capital		400						400
Profit and loss account		65						65
Long-term loan		200						200
Profit					198			198
Total	5,465	5,465	375	375	4,410	4,410	1,613	1,613

BPP PUBLISHING

(b) Draft a profit and loss account for the year ended 31 March 20X8 (after adjustments made in task (a)).

Note. You are *not* required to prepare a statement of total recognised gains and losses or the reconciliation of movements in shareholders' funds required under FRS 3.

(c) The directors have asked you a number of questions. Prepare notes to answer them referring to company law and accounting standards where appropriate.

 (i) An independent valuer has valued the land and buildings at £550,000. The directors have asked you if it is possible to show this valuation rather than the cost of the assets in the trial balance and, if so, to detail the entries needed to show the increased value of the fixed assets in the accounts.

 (ii) The directors understand that the accounts are prepared under the accruals concept. They are unsure what this means and have asked you to explain it briefly using one example from the accounts of Solu Ltd.

 (iii) The directors understand that Edward Ltd is now a subsidiary undertaking of Solu Ltd but they would like to have the definition of a subsidiary undertaking clarified. Define in simple terms a subsidiary undertaking according to FRS 2 *Accounting for subsidiary undertakings* and the Companies Act.

(d) Calculate the minority interest in the Solu Group as at 31 March 20X8.

35   BATHLEA (60 mins)   12/98

You work as an assistant accountant in an accountancy firm. Your manager has asked you to help with the preparation of the financial statements of Bathlea Ltd for the year ended 30 September 20X8. The company operates a warehouse which distributes computer components. The bookkeeper has provided you with the extended trial balance of Bathlea Ltd for the year ended 30 September 20X8, which is set out on page 58.

The following further information has been supplied.

(a) The authorised and issued share capital of the company consists of ordinary shares with a nominal value of £1.

(b) The company has paid an interim dividend of 3p per share. The company wishes to provide for a final dividend of 5.5p per share.

(c) The corporation tax charge for the year has been calculated as £11,000.

(d) Depreciation has been charged on all assets for the year and included in the trial balance figures for distribution costs and administrative expenses.

(e) The interest on the long-term loan is charged at 12% per annum and is paid monthly in arrears. The charge for the first eleven months of the year is included in the trial balance.

(f) A debtor owing Bathlea Ltd £10,000 went into liquidation on 2 October 20X8. This has not been accounted for.

(g) The general provision for bad debts is to be adjusted to 3% of debtors.

BATHLEA LIMITED: EXTENDED TRIAL BALANCE 30 SEPTEMBER 20X8

Description	Trial balance		Adjustments		Profit and loss account		Balance sheet	
	Debit £'000	Credit £'000	Debit £'000	Credit £'000	Debit £'000	Credit £'000	Debit £'000	Credit £'000
Land and buildings - cost	300						300	
Fixtures and fittings - cost	220						220	
Motor vehicles - cost	70						70	
Office equipment - cost	80						80	
Land and buildings - accumulated depreciation		65						65
Fixtures and fittings - accumulated depreciation		43						43
Motor vehicles - accumulated depreciation		27						27
Office equipment - accumulated depreciation		35						35
Sales		3,509				3,509		
Purchases	1,600				1,600			
Stock	200		250	250	200	250	250	
Debtors	370						370	
Provision for bad debts		5						5
Prepayments			10				10	
Bank overdraft		3						3
Creditors		350						350
Accruals				9				9
Carriage inwards	91				91			
Distribution costs	860		7	10	857			
Administrative expenses	890		2		892			
Interest charges	11				11			
Interim dividend	15				15			
Share capital		500						500
Profit and loss account		70						70
Long-term loan		100						100
Profit (loss)					93			93
Total	4,707	4,707	269	269	3,759	3,759	1,300	1,300

Tasks

(a) Make the necessary journal entries as a result of the further information given above. Dates and narratives are not required.

Notes

1   Ignore any effect of these adjustments on the tax charge for the year given above.

2   You must show any workings relevant to these adjustments.

(b) Draft a profit and loss account for the year ended 30 September 20X8 and a balance sheet as at that date (after adjustments made in task (a)).

(c) The directors have asked you a number of questions. Prepare notes to answer them referring to accounting standards were appropriate.

   (i)   There is a law suit pending against Bathlea Ltd. There is a remote possibility that it will result in Bathlea Ltd having to pay a customer compensation of £10,000 plus court costs. No account has been taken of this in the extended trial balance. The directors wish to know if it should be accrued.

   (ii)   The directors are considering quite a large development project next year and would like to know the possible alternative accounting treatments for this expenditure in next year's accounts.

36   CLAUDE (25 mins)   4/94

You have been asked to provide assistance to the accountant of Claude Ltd, a distributor of artists' materials, in finalising the cash flow statement for the year ended 31 December 20X3. The accountant has produced a draft cash flow statement which is set out below along with the profit and loss account and balance sheet for the year.

CLAUDE LIMITED
PROFIT AND LOSS ACCOUNT FOR THE YEAR ENDED 31 DECEMBER 20X3

	20X3		20X2	
	£'000	£'000	£'000	£'000
Turnover		5,625		4,931
Opening stock	613		543	
Purchases	3,252		2,872	
Closing stock	(719)		(613)	
Cost of sales		3,146		2,802
Gross profit		2,479		2,129
Depreciation		352		261
Other expenses		1,091		873
Loss on sale of fixed assets		75		31
Operating profit for the year		961		964
Interest payable		98		56
Profit before tax		863		908
Taxation on profit		305		321
Profit after tax		558		587
Ordinary dividend		106		84
Retained profit		452		503

CLAUDE LIMITED
BALANCE SHEET AS AT 31 DECEMBER 20X3

	20X3	20X2
	£'000	£'000
Fixed assets	3,046	1,857
Current assets		
Stocks	719	613
Debtors	722	523
Cash	-	299
	1,441	1,435
Current liabilities		
Trade creditors	501	452
Dividends payable	73	56
Taxation	305	321
Bank overdraft	353	-
	1,232	829
Net current assets	209	606
Long-term loan	1,230	990
	2,025	1,473
	£'000	£'000
Capital and reserves		
Called up share capital	500	400
Profit and loss account	1,525	1,073
	2,025	1,473

CLAUDE LIMITED
CASH FLOW STATEMENT FOR THE YEAR ENDED 31 DECEMBER 20X3

	£'000
Net cash inflow from operating activities	982
Returns on investments and servicing of finance	
Interest paid	(98)
Taxation	(321)
Capital expenditiure	
Payments to acquire tangible fixed assets	(1,634)
Sale of assets	168
	(903)
Equity dividends paid	(89)
Net cash outflow before financing	(992)
Financing	
Loan	240
Issue of ordinary share capital	100
Decrease in cash	(652)

Tasks

(a) Provide a reconciliation between cash flows from operating activities and operating profit for 20X3. (12 mins)

(b) The directors of Claude Ltd are not convinced that a cash flow statement has any value for the users of financial statements given that a balance sheet and profit and loss account have already been provided. Write a memo to the directors explaining what additional information is provided by the cash flow statement and what value such a statement would have for users of the financial statements. (13 mins)

One of the partners in your firm of accountants has asked you to assist the accountant of Bark Ltd, a distributor of garden compost, in the production of a cash flow statement for the year ended 31 March 20X4. The financial statements of Bark Ltd, produced by the company's bookkeeper for internal purposes, are set out below, along with some further information relating to the reporting year.

BARK LIMITED
PROFIT AND LOSS ACCOUNT FOR THE YEAR ENDED 31 MARCH

	20X4		*20X3*	
	£'000	£'000	£'000	£'000
Turnover		3,845		3,335
Opening stock	523		445	
Purchases	2,553		2,291	
Closing stock	(634)		(523)	
Cost of sales		2,442		2,213
Gross profit		1,403		1,122
Depreciation		253		228
Other expenses		446		395
Profit on sale of fixed assets		35		21
Operating profit for the year		739		520
Interest payable		66		86
Profit before tax		673		434
Taxation on profit		235		152
Profit after tax		438		282
Ordinary dividend		85		65
Retained profit		353		217

BARK LIMITED
BALANCE SHEET AS AT 31 MARCH

	20X4	*20X3*
	£'000	£'000
Fixed assets	1,774	1,340
Current assets		
Stocks	634	523
Debtors	463	461
Cash	-	63
	1,097	1,047
Current liabilities		
Trade creditors	447	575
Dividends payable	85	65
Taxation	186	132
Bank overdraft	103	-
	821	772
Net current assets	276	275
Long-term loan	523	541
	1,527	1,074
Capital and reserves		
Called up share capital	600	500
Profit and loss account	927	574
	1,527	1,074

Further information is as follows.

(a) Fixed assets costing £164,000 with accumulated depreciation of £98,000 were sold in the year for £101,000.

(b) All sales and purchases were on credit. Other expenses were paid for in cash.

Tasks

(a) Prepare a cash flow statement for Bark Ltd for the year ended 31 March 20X4 using the 'indirect method'. The revised FRS 1 format should be used (30 mins)

(b) Provide a reconciliation between cash flows from operating activities and operating profit. (15 mins)

38 FUN AND GAMES (40 mins) 12/98

The directors of Fun Ltd have a number of questions relating to the financial statements of their recently acquired subsidiary undertaking, Games Ltd. Fun Ltd acquired 75% of the ordinary share capital of Games Ltd on 30 September 20X8 for £2,244,000. The fair value of the fixed assets in Games Ltd as at 30 September 20X8 was £2,045,000. The directors have provided you with the balance sheet of Games Ltd as at 30 September 20X8 along with some further information.

GAMES LIMITED
BALANCE SHEET AS AT 30 SEPTEMBER 20X8

	20X8	20X7
	£'000	£'000
Fixed assets	1,845	1,615
Current assets		
Stocks	918	873
Trade debtors	751	607
Cash	23	87
	1,692	1,567
Current liabilities		
Trade creditors	583	512
Dividends payable	52	48
Taxation	62	54
	697	614
Net current assets	995	953
Long term loan	560	420
	2,280	2,148
Capital and reserves		
Called up share capital	1,000	1,000
Share premium	100	100
Profit and loss account	1,180	1,048
	2,280	2,148

Further information

(a) No fixed assets were sold during the year. The depreciation charge for the year amounted to £277,000.

(b) All sales and purchases were on credit. Other expenses were paid for in cash.

(c) The profit on ordinary activities before taxation was £246,000. Interest of £56,000 was charged in the year.

Tasks

(a) Provide a reconciliation between cash flows from operating activities and operating profit for Games Ltd for the year ended 30 September 20X8.

You are *not* required to prepare a cash flow statement.

(b) Prepare notes to take to the Board meeting to answer the following questions of the directors.

(i) What figure for the minority interest would appear in the consolidated balance sheet of Fun Ltd as at 30 September 1998?

(ii) Where in the balance sheet would the minority interest be disclosed?

(iii) What is a 'minority interest'?

39 GEORGE (30 mins)　　　　　　　　　　　　　　　　　　　　　　6/95

You have been given the following information about George Ltd for the year ending 31 March 20X5, with comparative figures for the year ending 31 March 20X4.

GEORGE LIMITED
PROFIT AND LOSS FOR THE YEAR ENDED 31 MARCH

	20X5		20X4	
	£'000	£'000	£'000	£'000
Turnover		2,500		1,775
Opening stock	200		100	
Purchases	1,500		1,000	
Closing stock	(210)		(200)	
Cost of sales		1,490		900
Gross profit		1,010		875
Depreciation		275		250
Other expenses		500		425
Profit on sales of fixed assets		2		-
Operating profit for the year		237		200
Interest paid		20		35
Profit before tax		217		165
Taxation on profit		25		21
Profit after tax		192		144
Proposed dividends		35		30
Retained profit		157		114

GEORGE LIMITED
BALANCE SHEET AS AT 31 MARCH

	20X5		20X4	
	£'000	£'000	£'000	£'000
Fixed assets		330		500
Current assets				
Stocks	210		200	
Debtors	390		250	
Cash	-		10	
	600		460	
Current liabilities				
Trade creditors	150		160	
Dividends payable	35		30	
Taxation	25		21	
Bank overdraft	199		-	
	409		211	
Net current assets		191		249
		521		749
Debentures				500
Long-term loan		200		100
		321		149
Capital and reserves				
Called up share capital		40		25
Profit and loss account		281		124
		321		149

Further information

(a) In May 20X4 an asset was sold which originally cost £10,000 and was purchased when the company was started up two years ago. A new asset was bought for £110,000 in June 20X4. Fixed assets are depreciated at 25% of cost. The policy is to charge a full year's depreciation in the year of purchase and none in the year of sale.

(b) Loan interest is charged at 10% per annum. The long-term loan was increased on 1 April 20X4.

(c) The 5% debentures were redeemed on 1 April 20X4.

(d) Sales and purchases were on credit. All other expenses, including interest due, were paid in cash.

(e) On 1 October 20X4 there was a new issue of shares. Fifteen thousand ordinary £1 shares were issued at par.

Tasks

(a) Prepare a cash flow statement for the period.

(b) Prepare a reconciliation between cash flows from operating activities and operating profit.

40   CASHEDIN (18 mins)   12/95

The bookkeeper of Cashedin Ltd has asked for your assistance in producing a cash flow statement for the company for the year ended 30 September 20X5 in accordance with FRS 1. He has derived the information which is required to be included in the cash flow statement, but is not sure of the format in which it should be presented. The information is set out below.

	£000s
Operating profit before tax	24
Depreciation charge for the year	318
Proceeds from sale of fixed assets	132
Issue of shares for cash	150
Cash received from new loan	200
Purchase of fixed assets for cash	358
Interest paid	218
Taxation paid	75
Dividends paid	280
Increase in stocks	251
Increase in debtors	152
Increase in creditors	165
Decrease in cash	345

Using the information provided by the bookkeeper given above, prepare a cash flow statement for Cashedin Ltd for the year ended 30 September 20X5 in accordance with the requirements of FRS 1. Show clearly your reconciliation between operating profit and net cash inflow from operating activities.

41   POISED (15 mins)   12/96

You have been asked to assist in the production of a reconciliation between cash flows from operating activities and operating profit for the year ended 31 July 20X6 for Poised Ltd. The financial statements of the company drafted for internal purposes are set out below, along with some further information relating to the reporting year.

POISED LIMITED
PROFIT AND LOSS ACCOUNT FOR THE YEAR ENDED 31 JULY 20X6

		20X6
		£000
Turnover		12,482
Opening stock	2,138	
Purchases	8,530	
Closing stock	(2,473)	
Cost of sales		8,195
Gross profit		4,287
Depreciation		1,347
Other expenses		841
Operating profit for the year		2,099
Interest paid		392
Profit before tax		1,707
Taxation on profit		562
Profit after tax		1,145
Ordinary dividend		360
Retained profit		785

POISED LIMITED
BALANCE SHEET AS AT 31 JULY 20X6

	20X6	20X5
	£000	£000
Fixed assets	6,867	6,739
Current assets		
Stocks	2,473	2,138
Trade debtors	1,872	1,653
Cash	1,853	149
	6,198	3,940
Current liabilities		
Trade creditors	1,579	1,238
Dividends payable	240	265
Taxation	562	477
	2,381	1,980
Net current assets	3,817	1,960
Long term loan	4,200	3,800
	6,484	4,899
Capital and reserves		
Called up share capital	3,000	2,500
Share premium	400	100
Profit and loss account	3,084	2,299
	6,484	4,899

Further information

(a) No fixed assets were sold during the year.

(b) All sales and purchases were on credit. Other expenses were paid for in cash.

Provide a reconciliation between cash flows from operating activities and operating profit for the year ended 31 July 20X6.

Note. You are *not* required to prepare a cash flow statement.

42   EDLIN (30 mins)   6/98

You have been given the financial statements of Edlin Ltd for the year ended 31 March 20X8, with comparative figures for the year ended 31 March 20X7. The company is expanding and is in the middle of a major programme of replacing all of its fixed assets.

EDLIN LIMITED
PROFIT AND LOSS ACCOUNT FOR THE YEAR ENDED 31 MARCH

	20X8		*20X7*	
	£'000	£'000	£'000	£'000
Turnover, continuing operations		3,000		2,000
Cost of sales: Opening stock	200		150	
Purchases	1,700		1,250	
Closing stock	(220)		(200)	
		1,680		1,200
Gross profit		1,320		800
Depreciation		175		150
Other expenses		500		400
Profit on sale of fixed asset		5		-
Operating profit for the year		650		250
Interest paid		15		12
Profit before tax		635		238
Taxation on profit		100		35
Profit after tax		535		203
Proposed dividends		100		50
Retained profit		435		153
Retained profit (loss) b/f		115		(38)
Retained profit c/f		550		115

EDLIN LIMITED
BALANCE SHEET AS AT 31 MARCH

	20X8		*20X7*	
	£'000	£'000	£'000	£'000
Fixed assets		552		200
Current assets				
Stock	220		200	
Debtors	250		160	
Cash	218		20	
	688		380	
Current liabilities				
Trade creditors	150		110	
Dividends payable	100		50	
Taxation	100		35	
	350		195	
Net current assets		338		185
Total assets less current liabilities		890		385
Long term liabilities				
Long-term loan		150		120
		740		265
Capital and reserves				
Called up share capital		120		100
Share premium account		70		50
Profit and loss account		550		115
		740		265

The following further information is provided.

(a) In July 20X7 an asset was sold which had originally cost £20,000 and was purchased by the company in July 20X4. Fixed assets are depreciated on a straight line basis at 20%. The policy is to charge a full year's depreciation in the year of purchase and none in the year of sale.

(b) A new asset was purchased for £535,000 during the year.

(c) Sales and purchases were on credit with all other expenses (including interest) being paid in cash.

(d) There was a share issue during the year.

Tasks

(a) Prepare a reconciliation between cash flows from operating activities and operating profit for the year ended 31 March 20X8.

(b) Prepare a cash flow statement for the year ended 31 March 20X8 in accordance with FRS 1 (revised).

(c) Calculate the gearing and current ratios for Edlin for 20X8 and 20X7 and briefly comment on the ratios.

43   PRACTICE QUESTION: RATIOS

The following are the summarised accounts for Carrow Ltd, a company with an accounting year ending on 30 September.

SUMMARISED BALANCE SHEETS AS AT 30 SEPTEMBER

	20X6		20X7	
	£'000	£'000	£'000	£'000
Tangible fixed assets (at cost less depreciation)		4,995		12,700
Current assets				
Stocks	40,145		50,455	
Debtors	40,210		43,370	
Cash at bank	12,092		5,790	
	92,447		99,615	
Creditors: amounts falling due within one year				
Trade creditors	32,604		37,230	
Taxation	2,473		3,260	
Proposed dividend	1,785		1,985	
	36,862		42,475	
Net current assets		55,585		57,140
Total assets less current liabilities		60,580		69,840
Creditors: amounts falling due after more than one year				
10% debenture 2006/2010		19,840		19,840
		40,740		50,000
Capital and reserves				
Called-up share capital of £0.25 per share		9,920		9,920
Profit and loss account		30,820		40,080
		40,740		50,000

SUMMARISED PROFIT AND LOSS ACCOUNTS
FOR THE YEAR ENDED 30 SEPTEMBER

	20X6	20X7
	£'000	£'000
Turnover	486,300	583,900
Operating profit	17,238	20,670
Interest payable	1,984	1,984
Profit on ordinary activities before taxation	15,254	18,686
Tax on profit on ordinary activities	5,734	7,026
Profit for the financial year	9,520	11,660
Dividends	2,240	2,400
Retained profit for the year	7,280	9,260
Retained profits brought forward	23,540	30,820
Retained profits carried forward	30,820	40,080

Task

Calculate, for each year, two ratios for each of the following user groups, which are of particular significance to them:

(a)   shareholders;

(b)   trade creditors;

(c)   internal management.

Guidance notes

1   This tutorial question simply asks for calculations. In a central assessment you would almost certainly be asked to comment on any changes revealed by your ratios.

2   You should target your answer to the requirement of the question. For example, shareholders are unlikely to be particularly interested in the current or quick ratio.

3   Do not simply show numbers in your calculations; show in words how the ratio is calculated. Remember that there are sometimes different ways of calculating a ratio; if the assessor understands the method you have used, he is more likely to give you credit.

44   PRACTICE QUESTION: RATIO JARGON

A managing director returns from a frustrating interview with the manager of the bank where the business has its account. He turns to you for advice stating:

'The bank manager told me that the working capital ratio is too low, and the gearing ratio too high. As far as I am concerned this is just meaningless jargon.'

Task

Briefly explain the bank manager's statement in words which the managing director will understand.

Guidance note

An important aspect of the accounting technician's role is to explain technical matters to the layman. This question should give you some practice.

45   BIMBRIDGE (30 mins)   12/98

Bimbridge Hospitals Trust has just lost its supplier of bandages. The company that has been supplying it for the last five years has gone into liquidation. The Trust is concerned to select a new supplier which it can rely on to supply it with its needs for the foreseeable future. You have been asked by the Trust managers to analyse the financial statements of a potential supplier of bandages. You have obtained the latest financial statements of the company, in summary, form which are set out on page 69.

PATCH LIMITED
SUMMARY PROFIT AND LOSS ACCOUNTS
FOR THE YEAR ENDED 30 SEPTEMBER 20X8

	20X8	20X7
	£'000	£'000
Turnover	2,300	2,100
Cost of sales	1,035	945
Gross profit	1,265	1,155
Expenses	713	693
Net profit before interest and tax	552	462

PATCH LIMITED
SUMMARY BALANCE SHEETS
AS AT 30 SEPTEMBER 20X8

	20X8		20X7	
	£'000	£'000	£'000	£'000
Fixed assets		4,764		5,418
Current assets				
Stocks	522		419	
Debtors	406		356	
Cash	117		62	
	1,045		837	
Current liabilities				
Trade creditors	305		254	
Taxation	170		211	
	475		465	
Net current assets		570		372
Long-term loan		(1,654)		(2,490)
		3,680		3,300
Share capital		1,100		1,000
Share premium		282		227
Profit and loss account		2,298		2,073
		3,680		3,300

You have also obtained the relevant industry average ratios which are as follows:

	20X8	20X7
Return on capital employed	9.6%	9.4%
Net profit percentage	21.4%	21.3%
Quick ratio/acid test	1.0:1	0.9:1
Gearing (debt/capital employed)	36%	37%

Task

Prepare a report for the managers of Bimbridge Hospitals Trust recommending whether or not to use Patch Ltd as a supplier of bandages. Use the information contained in the financial statements of Patch Ltd and the industry averages supplied.

Your answer should:

(a)   Comment on the company's profitability, liquidity and financial position
(b)   Consider how the company has changed over the two years
(c)   Include a comparison with the industry as a whole

The report should include calculation of the following ratios for the two years.

(a)   Return on capital employed
(b)   Net profit percentage
(c)   Quick ratio/acid test
(d)   Gearing

46 BINS (35 mins)   Specimen

You have been asked by the directors of Bins Ltd, a distributor of domestic and industrial refuse containers, to analyse the financial statements of a potential supplier. They have identified a company called Gone Ltd as a potential supplier of containers. They have obtained the latest financial statements of the company, in summary form, which are set out below:

GONE LIMITED
SUMMARY PROFIT AND LOSS ACCOUNTS
FOR THE YEAR ENDED 31 DECEMBER

	20X7	20X6
	£'000	£'000
Turnover	1,800	1,300
Cost of sales	1,098	715
Gross profit	702	585
Expenses	504	315
Net profit before interest and tax	198	270

GONE LIMITED
SUMMARY BALANCE SHEETS
AS AT 31 DECEMBER

	20X7		20X6	
	£'000	£'000	£'000	£'000
Fixed assets		3,463		1,991
Current assets	460		853	
Current liabilities	(383)		(406)	
Net current assets		77		447
Long-term loan		(1,506)		(500)
		2,034		1,938
Share capital		800		800
Revaluation reserve		164		164
Profit and loss account		1,070		974
		2,034		1,938

The industry average ratios are as follows.

	20X7	20X6
Return on capital employed	13.4%	13.0%
Gross profit percentage	44.5%	43.2%
Net profit percentage	23.6%	23.2%
Current ratio	2.0:1	1.9:1
Gearing	36%	34%

Task

Prepare a report for the directors recommending whether or not to use Gone Ltd as a supplier for Bins Ltd given the information contained in the financial statements and the industry averages supplied. Your answer should comment on the profitability, liquidity and the level of gearing in the company, and how they have changed over the two years, and compare it with the industry as a whole. The report should include calculation of the following ratios for the two years.

(a) Return on capital employed
(b) Gross profit percentage
(c) Net profit percentage
(d) Current ratio
(e) Gearing

47 ANIMALETS (50 mins)

Animalets plc is a large company with a number of subsidiaries. The group manufactures and distributes pet food and pet accessories. It is considering buying some shares in Superpet Ltd, a small company which makes toys and novelties for pets.

You have been given the financial statements for Superpet Ltd for the year ended 30 September 20X8.

SUPERPET LIMITED
PROFIT AND LOSS ACCOUNT FOR THE YEAR ENDED 30 SEPTEMBER 20X8

	20X8		20X7	
	£'000	£'000	£'000	£'000
Turnover, continuing operations		2,000		1,500
Cost of sales: opening stock	300		200	
purchases	900		800	
closing stock	(350)		(300)	
		850		700
Gross profit		1,150		800
Depreciation		65		50
Other expenses		132		118
Profit on sale of fixed asset		5		-
Operating profit for the year		958		632
Interest paid		10		7
Profit before tax		948		625
Taxation on profit		300		200
Profit after tax		648		425
Proposed dividends		180		100
Retained profit		468		325
Retained profit b/f		450		125
Retained profit c/f		918		450

SUPERPET LIMITED
BALANCE SHEET AS AT 30 SEPTEMBER 20X8

	20X8		20X9	
	£'000	£'000	£'000	£'000
Fixed assets		1,138		638
Current assets				
Stock	350		300	
Debtors	400		250	
Cash	120		60	
	870		610	
Current liabilities				
Trade creditors	190		148	
Dividends payable	180		100	
Taxation	300		200	
	670		448	
Net current assets		200		162
Total assets less current liabilities		1,338		800
Long term liabilities				
Long term loan		(100)		(70)
		1,238		730
Capital and reserves				
Called up share capital		220		200
Share premium account		50		30
Revaluation reserve		50		50
Profit and loss account		918		450
		1,238		730

Tasks

(a) Prepare a report to the directors of Animalets plc which considers Superpet's position and performance. Your report should be based on the following ratios only.

    (i)   Gross profit ratio
    (ii)   Current ratio
    (iii) Acid test (quick) ratio
    (iv) Gearing ratio

You are not expected to include recommendations in your report.

(b) The directors of Animalets want to know how much cash Superpet received from operating activities for the year ended 30 September 20X8. Prepare a reconciliation of operating profit to cash flow from operating activities for this period.

(c) The directors of Animalets are considering the following two options.

    (i)   The purchase of 30% of the share capital in Superpet, which would give the directors of Animalets significant influence over Superpet

or

    (ii)   The purchase of 75% of the share capital in Superpet, which would give the directors of Animalets dominant influence over Superpet

Either option would constitute a participating interest in Superpet.

Explain briefly how these two different options would be accounted for in the consolidated profit and loss account and balance sheet of the Animalets Group.

48   PRACTICE QUESTION: CONSOLIDATED FINANCIAL STATEMENTS

'The consolidation of financial statements hides rather than provides information.'

You are required to discuss this statement.

Guidance notes

1   A perusal of real financial statements should come in useful here.
2   Construct a plan and a coherent argument around the topic.
3   Watch your grammar, spelling and handwriting.

49   BATH (60 mins)

Bath Ltd acquired 80% of the ordinary share capital of Jankin Ltd on 1 January 20X1 for the sum of £153,000 and 60% of the ordinary share capital of Arthur Ltd on 1 July 20X1 for the sum of £504,000.

From the information given below you are required to prepare the consolidated balance sheet of Bath Ltd at 31 December 20X1.

Comparative figures, notes to the accounts and an auditor's report are not required.

Workings must be shown.

(a) The balance sheets of the three companies at 31 December 20X1 are set out below.

	Bath Limited £	Jankin Limited £	Arthur Limited £
Share capital			
Ordinary shares of £0.25 each	750,000	100,000	400,000
Share premium	15,000	-	-
Profit and loss account			
1 January 20X1	191,000	19,400	132,000
Retained profits for 20X1	37,000	3,000	54,000
Taxation	78,000	24,000	56,000
Creditors	162,000	74,400	149,000
Bank overdraft: Bank A	74,000	-	-
Depreciation			
Freehold property	9,000	-	40,000
Plant and machinery	87,000	39,000	124,600
Dividends proposed	30,000	15,000	24,000
Current account	-	9,800	-
	1,433,000	284,600	979,600

	Bath Limited £	Jankin Limited £	Arthur Limited £
Freehold property, at cost	116,000	-	200,000
Plant and machinery, at cost	216,000	104,000	326,400
Investments in subsidiaries			
Jankin Limited	153,000	-	-
Arthur Limited	504,000	-	-
Trade investment	52,000	-	-
Stocks and work in progress	206,000	99,000	294,200
Debtors	172,200	73,000	95,000
Bank balance: Bank B	-	7,900	62,800
Cash	1,100	700	1,200
Current account	12,700	-	-
	1,433,000	284,600	979,600

(b) No interim dividends were declared or paid in 20X1 out of 20X1 profits. Bath Ltd has not yet accounted for dividends receivable from its subsidiary companies.

(c) A remittance of £1,700 from Jankin Ltd in December 20X1 was not received by Bath Ltd until January 20X2.

(d) An invoice for £1,200 for stock material (including £240 profit) had been included in sales in 20X1 by Bath Ltd but it was not received by Jankin Ltd until 20X2.

(e) In Jankin Ltd's stock at 31 December 20X1, were goods to the value of £8,000 ex Bath Ltd on which the latter had taken profit of £1,600.

(f) Profits of Arthur Ltd are deemed to have accrued equally throughout the year.

(g) Any goodwill arising on consolidation is to be amortised over four years.

50 THOMAS (45 mins) 12/96

You have been asked to assist in the preparation of the consolidated accounts of the Thomas group. Set out below are the balance sheets of Thomas Ltd and James Ltd for the year ended 30 September 20X6.

BALANCE SHEET AS AT 30 SEPTEMBER 20X6

	Thomas Ltd	James Ltd
	£'000	£'000
Fixed assets	13,022	3,410
Investment in James Ltd	3,760	-
Current assets		
Stocks	6,682	2,020
Debtors	5,526	852
Cash	273	58
	12,481	2,930
Current liabilities		
Trade creditors	3,987	507
Taxation	834	173
	4,821	680
Net current assets	7,660	2,250
Total assets less current liabilities	24,442	5,660
Long-term loan	8,000	1,500
	16,442	4,160
Capital and reserves		
Called up share capital	5,000	1,000
Share premium	2,500	400
Profit and loss account	8,942	2,760
	16,442	4,160

You have been given the following further information.

(a) The share capital of both Thomas Ltd and James Ltd consists of ordinary shares of £1 each. There have been no changes to the balances during the year.

(b) Thomas Ltd acquired 800,000 shares in James Ltd on 30 September 20X5 at a cost of £3,760,000.

(c) At 30 September 20X5 the balance on the profit and loss account of James Ltd was £2,000,000.

(d) The fair value of the fixed assets of James Ltd at 30 September 20X5 was £3,910,000. The revaluation has not been reflected in the books of James Ltd.

(e) Goodwill arising on consolidation is considered to have an indefinite life and is to remain in the balance sheet.

Task

Prepare a consolidated balance sheet for Thomas Ltd and its subsidiary undertaking as at 30 September 20X6.

51 **ENTERPRISE AND VULCAN (50 mins)**

Enterprise plc purchased 30% of Vulcan Ltd on 1 July 20X4. At all times, Enterprise participates fully in Vulcan's financial and operating policy decisions. Goodwill is to be capitalised and amortised over five years.

EXTRACT FROM VULCAN LTD'S BALANCE SHEET AT ACQUISITION

	£'000
Share capital	2,000
Revaluation reserve	200
Profit and loss reserve	900
	3,100

BALANCE SHEETS AS AT 30 JUNE 20X8

	Enterprise plc group		Vulcan Ltd	
	£'000	£'000	£'000	£'000
Fixed assets				
Tangible fixed assets		8,000		7,000
Investment in therapy		2,000		-
		10,000		7,000
Current assets				
Stock	1,340		860	
Debtors	1,000		790	
Cash	260		430	
	2,600		2,080	
Creditors *(due within one year)*	(1,500)		(1,140)	
		1,100		940
		11,100		7,940
Capital and reserves				
Equity share capital		4,000		2,000
Revaluation reserve		2,000		1,000
Profit and loss reserve		5,100		4,940
		11,100		7,940

PROFIT AND LOSS ACCOUNTS FOR THE YEAR ENDING 30 JUNE 20X8

	Enterprise plc group	Vulcan Ltd
	£'000	£'000
Turnover	10,000	6,0000
Cost of sales	(6,000)	(3,000)
Gross profit	4,000	3,000
Expenses	(1,500)	(880)
Operating profit	2,500	2,120
Interest	(100)	(20)
Profit on ordinary activities before tax	2,400	2,100
Tax on ordinary activities	(800)	(700)
Profit on ordinary activities after tax	1,600	1,400
Dividends	(600)	(100)
Retained profit	1,000	1,300

Task

Prepare the consolidated balance sheet and P&L account for the year ended 30 June 20X8. Ignore any additional disclosure requirements of FRS 9.

52 SCENARIO: PAPIER MÂCHÉ (130 mins)   6/99
SECTION 1

Machier Ltd is a company that supplies stationery for business and domestic purposes. You have been asked to assist the directors in the interpretation of the financial statements of the company. They are intending to apply to the bank for a substantial loan. The bank has asked them for their financial statements for the last two years. The directors wish to know how the bank will view their profitability, liquidity and financial position on the evidence of these financial statements.

The directors are also concerned that they do not fully understand the financial statements of customers to whom they supply stationery. The customers include public sector and other not-for-profit organisations.

You have been supplied with the profit and loss account and the balance sheet of Machier Ltd for two years, prepared for internal purposes. These are set out below.

MACHIER LIMITED
PROFiT AND LOSS ACCOUNT AS AT 31 MARCH

	20X9	20X8
	£'000	£'000
Turnover	2,636	1,687
Cost of sales	923	590
Gross profit	1,713	1,097
Depreciation	856	475
Other expenses	126	101
Profit on the sale of fixed assets	7	2
Operating profit for the year	738	523
Interest paid	252	120
Profit before tax	486	403
Taxation on profit	165	137
Profit after tax	321	266
Ordinary dividend	40	20
Retained profit	281	246
Retained profit brought forward	1,127	881
Retained profit carried forward	1,408	1,127

MACHIER LIMITED
BALANCE SHEET AS AT 31 MARCH

	20X9	20X8
	£'000	£'000
Fixed assets	4,282	2,376
Current assets		
Stock	448	287
Debtors	527	337
Cash	-	86
	975	710
Current liabilities		
Trade creditors	381	212
Dividends payable	20	10
Taxation	165	137
Bank overdraft	183	-
	749	359
Net current assets	226	351
Long term loan	2,800	1,500
	1,708	1,227
Capital and reserves		
Called up share capital	200	100
Share premium	100	-
Profit and loss account	1,408	1,127
	1,708	1,227

Task 1.1

Prepare a report for the directors which includes the following:

(a) A calculation of the following ratios of Machier Ltd for the two years:

    (i) Return on equity
    (ii) Net profit percentage
    (iii) Quick ratio/acid test
    (iv) Gearing ratio
    (v) Interest cover

(b)   Comments on the profitability, liquidity and the financial position of the company as revealed by the ratios and a statement of how this had changed over the two years covered by the financial statements

(c)   An opinion as to whether the bank would be likely to give the company a substantial loan based solely on the information in the financial statements

Task 1.2

Prepare notes for the directors answering the following questions.

(a)   What are the elements in a balance sheet of a company? State which of the balances in the balance sheet of Machier Ltd fall under each element.

(b)   How are the elements related in the accounting equation? Show numerically that the accounting equation is maintained in the balance sheet of Machier Ltd.

(c)   What is the difference between an income and expenditure account for a not-for-profit organisation and a profit and loss account for a commercial company?

(d)   What is the equivalent of the capital balances in a not-for-profit organisation?

(e)   How, in general terms, do the uses of financial statements for commerical companies differ from those of not-for-profit organisations? Give one use of financial statements of a public sector or other not-for-profit organisations with which you are familiar.

SECTION 2

You are advised to spend approximately 75 minutes on this section.
This section is in two parts.

Part A

The directors of Machier Ltd have asked you to assist them in producing a cash flow statement for the year ended 31 March 20X9 using the information in the balance sheet and profit and loss account given in the data for Section 1.

The following further information is provided.

(a)   Fixed assets costing £28,000 with accumulated depreciation of £19,000 were sold in the year.

(b)   All sales and purchases were on credit. Other expenses were paid for in cash.

The directors have also been in negotiation with the directors of another company, Papier Ltd, about the possibility of Papier Ltd buying 75% of the share capital of Machier Ltd. If the acquisition goes ahead, Papier Ltd will pay £1,761,000 for the shares based on the value of the company at 31 March 20X9. The fair value of the fixed assets in Machier Ltd at 31 March 20X9, the agreed date of acquisition, is £4,682,000. All of the other assets and liabilities are stated at fair value. There is a meeting of the directors of both companies shortly. The directors of Machier Ltd wish you to attend this meeting to explain some of the accounting issues involved in the acqusition of Machier Ltd by Papier Ltd.

Task 2.1

Provide a reconciliation between cash flows from operating activities and operating profit of Machier Ltd for the year ended 31 March 20X9.

Task 2.2

Prepare a cash flow statement for Machier Ltd for the year ended 31 March 20X9 in accordance with the requirements of FRS 1 (Revised).

Task 2.3

Calculate the goodwill on consolidation that would arise on acqusition if Papier Ltd had purchased 75% of the shares in Machier Ltd on 31 March 20X9.

Note. You are *not* required to produce a consolidated balance sheet for the group.

Task 2.4

In a note to the directors, explain the options that are available for the accounting treatment of goodwill arising on acquisition in group accounts.

Part B

You have been assigned to assist in the preparation of the financial statements of Typeset Ltd for the year ended 31 March 20X9. The company is a wholsesale distributor of desktop publishing equipment. You have been provided with the extended trial balance of Typeset Ltd as at 31 March 20X9 which is set out on the next page.

You have been given the following further information.

(a) The authorised share capital of the business, all of which has been issued, consists of ordinary shares with a nominal value of £1.

(b) Depreciation has been calculated on a monthly basis on all of the fixed assets of the business and has already been entered into the distribution costs and administration expenses ledger balances as shown on the extended trial balance.

(c) The corporation tax charge for the year has been calculated as £493,000.

(d) The company has paid an interim dividend of 5p per share during the year but has not provided for the proposed final dividend of 7p per share.

(e) One of the customers who owed the company £36,000 at the end of the year is in financial difficulties. The directors have estimated that only half of this amount is likely to be paid. No adjustment has been made for this in the extended trial balance. The general provision for doubtful debts is to be maintained at 2% of the remaining debtors excluding the £36,000 balance.

Task 2.5

Making any adjustments required as a result of the further information provided, draft a balance sheet for Typeset Ltd as at 31 March 20X9.

Notes

1 You are not required to produce notes to the accounts.

2 You must show any workings relevant to understanding your calculation of figures appearnig in the financial statements.

3 You are not required to produce journal entries for any adjustments to the figures in the extended trial balance that are required.

4 You should ignore any effect of these adjustments on the tax charge for the year as given above.

TYPSET LIMITED

EXTENDED TRIAL BALANCE 31 MARCH 20X9

Description	Trial balance Debit £'000	Trial balance Credit £'000	Adjustments Debit £'000	Adjustments Credit £'000	Profit and loss account Debit £'000	Profit and loss account Credit £'000	Balance sheet Debit £'000	Balance sheet Credit £'000
Trade debtors	3,136						3,136	
Cash at bank	216						216	
Interest	125				125			
Profit and loss account		3,533						3,533
Provision for doubtful debts		37		36				37
Distribution costs	3,549		59		3,572			
Administrative expenses	3,061		63	61	3,063			
Revaluation reserve		500						500
Sales		18,757				18,757		
Land – cost	2,075						2,075	
Buildings – cost	2,077						2,077	
Fixtures and fittings – cost	1,058						1,058	
Motor vehicles – cost	2,344						2,344	
Office equipment – cost	533						533	
Stock	3,921		4,187	4,187	3,921	4,187	4,187	
Purchases	10,582				10,582			
Interim dividend	250				250			
Trade creditors		1,763						1,763
Buildings – accumulated depreciation		383						383
Fixtures and fittings – accumulated depreciation		495						495
Motor vehicles – accumulated depreciation		1,237						1,237
Office equipment – accumulated depreciation		152						152
Prepayments			97				97	
Odinary share capital		5,000						5,000
Share premium		1,200						1,200
Accruals				122				122
Investments	1,580						1,580	
Long-term loan		1,450						1,450
Profit					1,431			1,431
TOTAL	34,507	34,507	4,406	4,406	22,944	22,944	17,303	17,303

BPP PUBLISHING

DECEMBER 1999 CENTRAL ASSESSMENT

(REVISED STANDARDS)

TECHNICIAN STAGE - NVQ4

UNIT 11
DRAFTING FINANCIAL STATEMENTS
(Accounting Practice,
Industry and Commerce)

Time allowed - 3 hours
Plus 15 minutes' reading time
Answer **all** questions

**DO NOT OPEN THIS PAPER UNTIL YOU ARE READY TO START
UNDER TIMED CONDITIONS**

This central assessment is in TWO sections. You are remined that competance must be achieved in both sections. You should therefore attempt and aim to complete EVERY task in EACH section.

SECTION 1

You are advised to spend approximately 55 minutes on this section.

This section is in two parts.

Part A

Task 1.1

The Accounting Standards Board's *Statement of Principles for Financial Reporting* states that:

> 'The objective of financial statements is to provide information about the reporting entity's financial performance and financial position that is useful to a wide range of users for assessing the stewardship of management and for making economic decisions.'

Illustrate this objective by:

(a) Selecting one external user of financial statements from either profit-making organisations or public sector/not-for-profit organisations and showing how it uses financial statements to assess the stewardship of management

(b) Selecting one external user of financial statements from either profit-making organisations or public sector/not-for-profit organisations and showing how it uses financial statements to make economic decisions

Part B

Data

Jonathan Fisher is intending to invest a substantial sum of money in a company. A colleague has suggested to him that he might want to invest in a private company called Carp Ltd which supplies pond equipment to retail outlets. You have been asked to assist him in interpreting the financial statements of the company which are set out below.

CARP LIMITED
SUMMARY PROFIT AND LOSS ACCOUNT FOR THE YEAR ENDED 30 SEPTEMBER

	1999	*1998*
	£'000	*£'000*
Turnover	3,183	2,756
Cost of sales	1,337	1,020
Gross profit	1,846	1,736
Expenses	1,178	1,047
Net profit before interest and tax	668	689
Interest	225	92
Profit before tax	443	597
Taxation	87	126
Profit after tax	356	471
Dividends	42	50
Retained profit	314	421

CARP LIMITED
SUMMARY BALANCE SHEETS AS AT 30 SEPTEMBER

	1999		1998	
	£'000	£'000	£'000	£'000
Fixed assets		4,214		2,030
Current assets				
Stock	795		689	
Debtors	531		459	
Cash	15		136	
	1,341		1,284	
Current liabilities				
Trade creditors	709		435	
Proposed dividend	42		50	
Taxation	87		126	
	838		611	
Net current assets		503		673
Long-term loan		(2,500)		(1,000)
		2,217		1,703
Share capital		700		500
Profit and loss account		1,517		1,203
		2,217		1,703

Task 1.2

Prepare notes for Jonathan Fisher covering the following points.

(a) Explain what a 'balance sheet' is and what a 'profit and loss account' is and identify the elements that appear in each statement.

(b) Explain the 'accounting equation' and demonstrate that the balance sheet of Carp Ltd as at 30 September 1999 conforms to it.

(c) Calculate the following ratios for the two years.

   (i)   Gearing
   (ii)   Net profit percentage
   (iii) Current ratio
   (iv)   Return on equity

(d) Using the ratios calculated, comment on the company's profitability, liquidity and financial position and consider how these have changed over the two years.

(e) Using only the calculation of the ratios and the analysis of the changes over the two years, state whether the company is a better prospect for investment in 1999 than it was in 1998. Give reasons for your answer.

SECTION 2

You are advised to spend approximately 125 minutes on this section.

This section is in four parts.

Part A

Data

You have been asked to assist in the preparation of the consolidated accounts of the Shopan Group. Set out below on the balance sheets of Shopan Ltd and its subsidiary undertaking Hower Ltd, as at 30 September 1999.

BALANCE SHEETS AS AT 30 SEPTEMBER 1999

	Shopan Limited		Hower Limited	
	£'000	£'000	£'000	£'000
Fixed assets		6,273		1,633
Investment in Hower Ltd		2,100		
Current assets				
Stock	1,901		865	
Debtors	1,555		547	
Cash	184		104	
	3,640		1,516	
Current liabilities				
Trade creditors	1,516		457	
Taxation	431		188	
	1,947		645	
Net current assets		1,693		871
Long-term loan		(2,870)		(400)
		7,196		2,104
Capital and reserves		2,000		500
Called up share capital		950		120
Share premium		4,246		1,484
Profit and loss account		7,196		2,104

Further information

(a)   The share capital of both Shopan Ltd and Hower Ltd consists of ordinary shares of £1 each.

(b)   Shopan Ltd acquired 375,000 shares in Hower Ltd on 30 September 1999.

(c)   The fair value of the fixed assets of Hower Ltd at 30 September 1999 was £2,033,000.

Task 2.1

Prepare a consolidated balance sheet for Shopan Ltd and its subsidiary undertaking as at 30 September 1999.

Task 2.2

FRS 2 states that 'a parent undertaking should prepare consolidated financial statements for its group'. Give two of the criteria that, according to FRS 2, determine whether an undertaking is the parent undertaking of another undertaking.

BPP
PUBLISHING

Part B

Data

A colleague has asked you to take over the drafting of a cash flow statement for Diewelt Ltd for the year ended 30 September 1999. Your colleague has already drafted a reconciliation between cash flows from operating activities and operating profit for the period. The financial statements of the company, drafted for internal purposes, along with the reconciliation are set out below, together with some further information relating to the reporting year.

DIEWELT LIMITED
PROFIT AND LOSS ACCOUNT FOR THE YEAR ENDED SEPTEMBER 1999

	1999
	£'000
Turnover	9,804
Cost of sales	5,784
Gross profit	4,020
Profit on sale of fixed asset	57
Depreciation	985
Other expenses	819
Operating profit for the year	2,273
Interest paid	365
Profit before tax	1,908
Taxation on profit	583
Profit after tax	1,325
Ordinary dividend	440
Retained profit	885

DIEWELT LIMITED
BALANCE SHEET AS AT 30 SEPTEMBER 1999

	1999		1998	
	£'000	£'000	£'000	£'000
Fixed assets		6,490		5,620
Current assets				
Stock	3,151		2,106	
Trade debtors	2,314		1,470	
Cash	103		383	
	5,568		3,959	
Current liabilities				
Trade creditors	964		1,034	
Dividends payable	264		192	
Taxation	583		491	
	1,811		1,717	
Net current assets		3,757		2,242
Long-term loan		(3,300)		(2,900)
		6,947		4,962
Capital and reserves		2,200		1,600
Called up share capital		800		300
Profit and loss account		3,947		3,062
		6,947		4,962

Further information

(a)   A fixed asset which had cost £136,000 and had accumulated depreciation of £85,000 was sold during the year.

(b)   All sales and purchases were on credit. Other expenses were paid for in cash.

RECONCILIATION OF OPERATING PROFIT
TO NET CASH INFLOW FROM OPERATING ACTIVITIES

	£'000
Operating profit	2,273
Depreciation charges	985
Profit on sale of tangible fixed assets	(57)
Increase in stock	(1,045)
Increase in debtors	(844)
Decrease in creditors	(70)
Net cash inflow from operating activities	1,242

Task 2.3

Prepare a cash flow statement for Diewelt Ltd for the year ended 30 September 1999 in accordance with the requirements of FRS 1 (Revised).

Part C

Data

Elizabeth Ogier has asked you to assist in the preparation of the year end financial statements of her business. She operates a wholesale perfume business. The trial balance as at 30 September 1999 is set out below.

BPP PUBLISHING

ELIZABETH OGIER

TRIAL BALANCE AS AT 30 SEPTEMBER 1999

	Debit £	Credit £
Purchases	113,565	
Rent, rates and insurance	8,291	
Motor expenses	5,813	
Bad debts	1,420	
Drawings	24,000	
Trade debtors	38,410	
Trade creditors		18,928
Capital as at 1 October 1998		83,707
Sales		230,461
Returns outwards		2,911
Carriage inwards	1,256	
Returns inwards	3,053	
Carriage outwards	1,571	
Salesperson's commission	2,561	
Bank charges	710	
Depreciation – office equipment	2,312	
Depreciation – fixtures and fittings	602	
Stock as at 1 October 1998	46,092	
Motor vehicles at cost	36,000	
Office equipment at cost	11,560	
Fixtures and fittings at cost	6,019	
Accumulated depreciation – motor vehicles		18,360
Accumulated depreciation – office equipment		3,825
Accumulated depreciation – fixtures and fittings		1,352
Wages, salaries and National Insurance contribution	47,564	
Lighting and heating	3,056	
Postage and stationery	1,037	
Telephone	3,571	
Cash at bank	2,131	
Cash in hand	102	
Accruals		1,562
Discounts allowed	410	
	361,106	361,106

Further information

(a) The stock at the close of business on 30 September 1999 was valued at cost at £49,477. However, included in this balance were some goods which had cost £8,200 but it is estimated that they could now be sold for only £4,800.

(b) Included in the rent, rates and insurance balance is a payment of £1,200 which relates to rent for the period from 1 October 1999 to December 1999.

(c) The purchases figure includes goods to the value of £2,000 which Elizabeth took from the business for personal use and for gifts to friends.

(d) Although depreciation for office equipment and fixtures and fittings has been calculated and charged for the year, no depreciation has been calculated or charged for motor vehicles. Motor vehicles are depreciated using the reducing balance method at a rate of 30% per annum.

Task 2.4

Make any additional adjustments you feel necessary to the balances in the trial balance as a result of the matters set out in the further information above. Set out your adjustments in the form of journal entries.

Note. Narratives are not required.

Task 2.5

Draft a profit and loss account for the year ended 30 September 1999.

Task 2.6

Draft a letter to Elizabeth justifying any adjustment you have made to:

(a)   The stock valuation on 30 September 1999

(b)   The balances in the trial balance as a result of Elizabeth taking goods out of the business for her personal use or for gifts to friends.

Your explanations should make reference, where relevant, to accounting concepts, accounting standards or generally accepted accounting principles.

Part D

Data

Geoffrey Thomas, Victoria Bologna and Albertine Rosario are in partnership together and own a florist shop. The partners have decided that they would each like to set up their own business and are thinking of dissolving the partnership. They wish to know how much profit they are entitled to for the year ended 30 September 1999. They have asked you to assist in the production of an appropriation account for the partnership.

They have given you the following information.

(a)   The profit-sharing ratios of the partnership are:

Geoffrey	6/10
Victoria	3/10
Albertine	1/10

(b)   The profit for the year ended 30 September 1999 amounted to £115,960.

(c)   Interest on capital is to be paid at a rate of 8% on the balance at the year end on the capital accounts. No interest is paid on the current accounts.

(d)   The partners are entitled to the following salaries per annum.

Geoffrey	£25,000
Victoria	£19,000
Albertine	£15,000

(e)   Cash drawings against these salaries during the year amounted to:

Geoffrey	£22,500
Victoria	£16,300
Albertine	£13,400

(f)   The balances on the capital accounts at the end of the year were as follows.

        Geoffrey   £56,000
        Victoria   £23,000
        Albertine   £8,000

Task 2.7

Prepare an appropriation account for the partnership for the year ended 30 September 1999.

Answers

1 OBJECTIVES

(a) The ASB *Statement of Principles* (Chapter 1) sets out the objectives of financial reporting.

Financial reporting has the objectives of providing information regarding the financial position, performance and financial adaptability of an entity.

The provision of such information will enable the various users of financial statements to take better informed decisions on economic matters such as investment planning .

The financial reporting package is also designed to provide information regarding the stewardship activities of the managers of a business to its owners. For limited companies, such information is required by law to be produced in a form prescribed by the Companies Act.

(b) The user groups identified by the ASB *Statement of Principles* were as follows.

    (i)   Public
    (ii)   Investors
    (iii) Lenders
    (iv) Government and other agencies
    (v)   Employees
    (vi) The Suppliers and other creditors
    (vii) Customers

(c) The information needs of each group are as follows.

Investors need data to enable investment decisions (buy, sell, hold) to be taken. The provision of information regarding stewardship is also important.

Lenders will need to know the financial position of a business in order to judge security and the ability of the business to repay the interest or capital. Decisions will also be needed regarding the ability of a business to handle an increased level of borrowings.

The government will need information to compile national statistics, to determine taxation liabilities and to assess applications for financial support received from companies. The compilation of data of regarding national economic performance will be helped by having a financial reporting package presented in a consistent manner by a variety of contributors.

Employees will need information to take decisions regarding employment prospects, stability of employers and to enable wage demands to be formulated. Bonus payments are also usually linked to reported performance levels

The public will want to know the relationship of the reporting entity with the community within which it operates, eg its contribution to the local economy. Increasingly, environmental issues are of concern as well.

Suppliers will need information in order to assess requests for lines of trade credit and the ability of their creditors to pay up on time.

Customers will need reassurance that an entity is sufficiently stable to satisfy their order on time and to specification. They will also use the reporting package to help to select a supplier.

(d) This a very wide ranging question.

Clearly no single reporting package can completely meet all the diverse needs discussed above, so what has emerged is something of a compromise. Traditionally, the view has been that provided the needs of shareholders are met, then the reporting package will also have gone a long way towards satisfying other users needs.

However, recent reporting developments such as summary financial statements, employee reports and environmental reports have gone some way to meeting the needs of specific user groups and this trend will no doubt continue.

Financial reporting is gradually moving towards satisfying the information needs of other user groups. However, financial reports are becoming ever more complex and some would say that they are increasingly difficult for non financially orientated users to deal with.

The final point is that the financial reporting package is essentially historical and is generally of only limited use in assessing the current or future status of an entity unless used in conjunction with other sources of information.

2   FUNDAMENTAL

(a) The four concepts are as follows:

Accruals. Income is matched with related expenditure in order to determine profits, therefore income and expenditure figures will include receivable and payable items which will also appear in the balance sheet as debtors and creditors. The financial statements therefore do not only reflect the results of settled cash transactions.

Prudence. Where alternative treatments or presentations of financial data are possible the financial statements should always reflect the most cautious presentation of the results. Profits should not be anticipated but losses should be recognised as they become apparent.

Going concern. The financial statements will be drawn up on the assumption that the entity will continue in existence for the foreseeable future and that there is no intention to curtail its operations.

Consistency. Similar items in a single reporting package should be given similar treatments. Also the treatments used in one period should be applied in the next unless there is a valid and disclosed reason to change. Valid comparisons can then be made and trends identified.

There is a presumption in financial reporting that these concepts have been applied if this is not the case then the facts must be disclosed.

(b) An example of conflict would be between accruals and prudence.

If a company enters into a contract to provide a service over a number of years, it is normal practice to accrue profit arising over the duration of the contract. However, future profits may be uncertain.

The accruals concept would say that the costs of providing the service should be matched with the revenue arising. Prudence would dictate that a cautious approach to the measurement of profit should be taken and that provisions for future losses should be recognised.

Where there is a conflict between the application of accruals and prudence, generally prudence will prevail.

(c) The two most important characteristics would be relevance and reliability if the information is to be useful.

Relevant information is that which is directed at satisfying users' information needs helping them to make, confirm or evaluate decisions which have to be made or which were previously made.

Reliable information means that the decisions can be taken using data which is free from error and which does not contain any bias. The information will faithfully reflect the facts.

It would be easy to produce information which is perhaps more relevant to users' needs but which is as a consequence less reliable. An example of this would be the publication of forecast financial information as part of the reporting package, useful but perhaps not very accurate.

3 ASSETS

> **Tutorial note**. The definitions of assets and liabilities in the ASB *Statement of Principles* are the key to answering this question .

(a) An asset can be defined as something valuable which a business owns or has the use of. This definition is, however, insufficiently precise because some assets are held for use over a long term whereas others may be consumed over a shorter period. Another problem is that an asset can be used when it is not owned by the business. Assets may also be tangible or intangible.

As you can see it is not so easy to define an asset after all!

The ASB defines assets as 'rights or other access to future economic benefits controlled by an entity as a result of past transactions or events'.

Fixed assets will enable the future economic benefits to accrue over a longer period covering the useful economic life of the assets.

Current assets will be consumed in earning profits in the shorter term.

Note that for both fixed and current assets ownership is not necessary in order for an item to meet the definition of an asset. The ability to control the use of the item to enjoy the economic benefits clearly is, however.

Liabilities are obligations to transfer economic benefits as a result of past transactions or events. The key word here is 'obligations'. The absence of an obligation means that a liability should not be recognised; this makes the recognition of items such as provisions and contingencies more difficult to determine because the point at which a liability emerges is often unclear.

(b) A fixed asset should initially be recognised when there is sufficient evidence that fixed assets have changed as result of an item and that a future monetary benefit will arise either through income or cost savings. Such benefits must be capable of being measured reliably in monetary terms.

When an asset is subsequently revalued similar criteria apply to the recognition of the remeasurement.

Note that assets should be derecognised when there is evidence that the entity no longer has the right to enjoy the future economic benefits from using the asset.

(c) Items which are hired by a business will only be recognised as fixed assets when the business can control the use of the asset, existing assets have clearly changed and there is a measurable economic benefit.

However, the nature of a hire contract is that it is usually for a fairly short period (unless it is a hire purchase contract). While the business may control the use of the hired asset in the short term, its owner has not fully transferred the rights and rewards of ownership to the current user, therefore recognition as a fixed asset is inappropriate.

The hire charges will be accounted for as an expense in the profit and loss account because they will result in a decrease in the ownership interests as result of reducing profits.

4 ORGANISATION

Tutorial note. You were asked for only one example – our answer gives three for completeness. Other reasonable types of organisation and user would also be acceptable.

(a) (i) *Profit making organisation*

Type of organisation	Example of user
Sole trader	Supplier
Partnership	Bank
Limited company	Shareholder

Not-for-profit organisation

Type of organisation	Example of user
Charity	Sponsor, person making donations
Club/society	Member
Local authority	Council tax payer
National Health Service Trusts	Department of Health

(ii) *Profit making organisation*

User	Possible decisions
Supplier	Whether to carry on supplying goods on credit (eg by looking at liquidity position)
Bank	Whether to continue an overdraft facility (by assessing profitability and liquidity
Shareholders	Whether to increase or decrease holding or whether to remove directors. They will assess liquidity, profitability, gearing and the stewardship of management.

Not-for-profit organisation

User	Possible decisions
Sponsor, person making donations	Whether the donations have been put to good use, eg is too much spent on administration?
Member	Whether the club has been efficiently run and whether the interests of all the members are being served.
Council tax payer	Whether the Local Authority has given value for money. Whether there are too many bad debts.
Department of health	Has the trust been efficiently run? Again, is too much being spent on administration?

(b) (i) Each of the items in the accounting equation is defined in the ASB's *Statement of Principles*.

    (1) *Assets* are 'rights or other access to future economic benefits controlled by an entity as a result of past transactions or events'.

(2) *Liabilities* are 'obligations of an entity to transfer economic benefits as a result of past transactions or events'.

(3) *Ownership interest* is the residual amount found by deducting all of the entity's liabilities from all of the entity's assets.

More simply, assets are owned by an entity, liabilities are owed by an entity and ownership interest is capital, which is owed to the owner.

(ii) (1) In the balance sheet of a *profit making organisation*, for example, a limited company, the ownership interest section would consist of share capital (originally paid in by the owners) and reserves (profits made by the company and owed to the owners.

(2) In the balance sheet of a *not-for-profit organisation*, such as a club, you will find an accumulated fund. This will be made up of capital introduced and accumulated surpluses of income over expenditure and is to be applied to further the organisations aims. In central government accounts, these funds are likely to be earmarked for specific purposes.

5 PRIMARY FINANCIAL STATEMENTS

(a) The primary statements are:

(i) The balance sheet
(ii) The profit and loss account
(iii) The statement of total recognised gains and losses (STRGL)
(iv) The cash flow statement

(b) The balance sheet sets out the financial position of the business at a point in time. Changes in owners' equity will be as a result of profits or losses (from the P & L account), the results of other recognised gains such as revaluations (from the STRGL) and contributions from or distributions to owners.

The profit and loss account contains the results of realised gains and losses in the period.

The STRGL brings together all the recognised gains and losses which may be realised or unrealised.

When a transaction occurs which results in the realisation of a previously recognised gain or loss, the effects will be seen partially in the P&L account and partially as a movement on reserves.

The STRGL thus provides a useful link between the P & L account and the balance sheet.

The P & L account uses the accruals concept to measure the effects of transactions whereas the cash flow statement provides a more objective measure of business performance and management of liquidity and debt. The cash flow statement thus explains changes in liquidity and debt between successive balance sheets and focuses upon the way in which cash is generated from operations and in other ways.

(c) Charities are 'not for profit' organisations (although some of their activities may be profit related). Their objectives are therefore fundamentally different, being aimed at meeting the objectives of the charity instead of maximising shareholder wealth and profits.

However, many charities are registered as limited companies and must comply with normal reporting practices so all the primary financial statements must be produced even though they may not be directly relevant to the charities' objectives.

Many charities operate using donated funds and is important that they are accountable for the use of these funds, so regulation is important.

The information needs of the users of charity accounts may be different from a normal investor, and arguably the primary financial statements do not adequately satisfy these needs. Charities operate in a very competitive market for donated funds these days and must be careful to report in such a way as to be readily understandable and to communicate the achievement of their objectives clearly if they are to continue to attract funds. Additional reports beyond the normal primary statements will be needed to fully explain the results for a period.

(d) The information needs of a member of the public will include matters such as the following.

(i) Social responsibility of organisations
(ii) Employment practices
(iii) Labour relations issues
(iv) Future prospects
(v) Environmental issues
(vi) Assistance to local interest groups (donations etc)
(vii) Impact upon the local and national economy

Clearly, the primary financial statements do not really help in meeting these needs and additional supplementary reports are required.

6 OBJECTIVE AND ELEMENTS

(a) The objective of financial statements has been set out in the ASB's *Statement of Principles* as follows.

> 'To provide information about the financial position, performance and financial adaptability of an enterprise that is useful to a wide range of users for assessing the stewardship of management and for making economic decisions.'

Whether financial statements meet this objective in all cases is debatable.

(b) An obvious example of a profit-making organisation is a *limited company*. One of the financial statements, the balance sheet, exists to provide information about the company's financial position, for example what it owns (assets) and what it owes (liabilities). The balance sheet also gives an indication of financial adaptability, for example whether the company has sufficient cash to settle debts if required. Information about financial performance is given in the profit and loss account.

Not-for-profit organisations, for example, clubs and societies have different objectives. They will not be concerned with performance as such, but with stewardship, ie have the resources of the club been used to achieve the club's objectives. In practice the club may well make a surplus of income over expenditure and will certainly not want to be making losses. As far as the financial position of the club is concerned, the balance sheet will provide the appropriate information.

Public sector bodies have different objectives. A local council, for example, exists to provide services to the public rather than to make a profit. Nevertheless, resources must be managed economically, efficiently and effectively and financial statements will give council tax payers an indication of whether this is happening.

(c) The elements of financial statements are identified in Chapter 4 of the *Statement of Principles* as follows.

(i)	Assets	(vi)	Gains
(ii)	Liabilities	(vii)	Losses
(iii)	Ownership interest	(viii)	Contributions from owners
(iv)	Income	(ix)	Distributions to owners
(v)	Expenditure		

(d) The elements of financial statements are interrelated in the profit and loss account and balance sheet by means of the accounting equation:

Assets – Liabilities = Ownership interest

(Ownership interest is also, in the accounts of a profit-making organisation, known as 'capital'.)

The change in ownership interest is equal to the profit for the accounting period plus contributions from owners (capital introduced) less distributions to owners (drawings and dividends).

Profit is, in effect, gains less losses. Some gains and losses are recorded in the profit and loss account and others in the statement of total recognised gains and losses, but the relationship of the elements is the same.

(e) In a public sector or not-for-profit organisation the term 'capital' is not used; instead we talk about a 'fund' or, sometimes, an 'accumulated fund'. A fund may be established for a particular purpose such as renewal of assets; alternatively it may serve a similar role to the capital accumulated in the accounts of a profit making organisation. For example a surplus of income over expenditure is added to a fund in the same way as a profit is added to capital. The main difference, however, is that, in a profit making organisation, capital is regarded as being 'owed to the owners'. This does not apply in a non profit making organisation.

7 PRACTICE QUESTION: COUNTRY CRAFTS

Workings

1 *Profit on sale of fixed asset account*

	£
Profit on van	950
Loss on car	700
Net profit	250

2 *Insurance claim*
Cost of damaged stock (mark up 100%) = 50% × £2,300
= £1,150 (a credit to the purchases account)
Less £200 excess = £950
Note. £200 is a 'stock loss' not covered by insurance.

3 *Stock write off*

Baby Beatrice mugs:	Cost 320/2	= £160
	NRV	= £120

∴ NRV below cost ∴ write off necessary

Windsor fire damage plate:	Cost 620/2	= £310
	NRV	= £350

No write off necessary, NRV above cost

4 *Bad debt expense/provision*

Provision required:	5% × £144,280 = £7,214

JOURNAL		Page 20
Details	**DR** **£**	**CR** **£**
(a) (i) Motor vans (cost) a/c	22,600	
Motor vans (cost) a/c		16,200
Motor vans (provision for dep'n) a/c (£16,000 × 25% × 3)	12,150	
Suspense a/c		17,600
Profit on sale of fixed asset a/c		950
Being purchase of van L673 NFU, transfer of provision for dep'n and sale of van H247 AFE in part exchange		
(ii) Suspense a/c	3,900	
Motor cars (cost) a/c		9,200
Motor cars (provision for dep'n) a/c (£9,200 × 25% × 2)	4,600	
Profit on sale of fixed asset a/c	700	
Being disposal of motor car J168 TFE at a loss		
(iii) Sales	250	
Sundry income		250
Being transfer of sundry income into correct account		

5   *Prepayments and accruals*

Rent: prepayment = $8/12 \times £7,488 = £4,992$
Electricity: bill for 3 months to February 20X4 = $2 \times £315 = £630$
$\therefore$ Accrual for December = $1/3 \times £630 = £210$

The solution to part (a) of this question is on page 100. Parts (b) to (d) are shown below.

	LEDGER BALANCES		ADJUSTMENTS		PROFIT AND LOSS A/C		BALANCE SHEET BALANCES	
	DEBIT	CREDIT	DEBIT	CREDIT	DEBIT	CREDIT	DEBIT	CREDIT
	£	£	£	£	£	£	£	£
Motor vans (cost)	42,400						42,400	
Motor cars (cost)	9,200						9,200	
Office furniture (cost)	4,850						4,850	
Computer equipment (cost)	16,830						16,830	
Motor vans (prov for dep'n)		4,950		10,600				15,550
Motor cars (prov for dep'n)		4,600		2,300				6,900
Office furniture (prov for dep'n)		1,940		485				2,425
Computer equipment (prov for dep'n)				5,610				5,610
Stock	24,730				24,730	31,600	31,600	
Debtors control	144,280						144,280	
Bank		610		43				653
Cash	50		43	43			50	
Creditors control		113,660						113,660
Sales		282,240				282,240		
Purchases	152,140			1,150	150,990			
Rent	12,480			4,992	7,488			
Heat and light	1,840		210		2,050			
Wages and salaries	75,400				75,400			
Office expenses	7,900		43		7,943			
Motor expenses	14,890				14,890			
Dep'n (motor vans)			10,600		10,600			
Dep'n (motor cars)			2,300		2,300			
Dep'n (office furniture)			485		485			
Dep'n (computer equipment)			5,610		5,610			
Share capital		50,000						50,000
Profit and loss		35,850						35,850
VAT		12,640						12,640
Profit on sale of fixed asset		250				250		
Sundry income		250				250		
Insurance claim			950				950	
Stock loss			200		200			
Bad debt expense			7,214		7,214			
Provision for doubtful debts				7,214				7,214
Prepayments			4,992				4,992	
Accruals				210				210
Profit					4,440			4,440
	506,990	506,990	32,647	32,647	314,340	314,340	255,152	255,152

BPP
PUBLISHING

8   TAYLORIANA

(a)   TAYLORIANA
PROFIT AND LOSS ACCOUNT FOR THE YEAR ENDED 31 MARCH 20X5

	£'000	£'000
Sales	257,350	
Less returns inwards	3,350	
		254,000
Cost of sales		
Opening stock	43,700	
Purchases	162,430	
Carriage inwards	1,320	
Less returns outwards	(7,460)	
	20X	
Less closing stock	(49,300)	
		150,690
		103,310
Less expenses		
Wages	39,420	
Depreciation: fixtures and fittings	2,800	
motor vehicles	4,100	
Bad debts (540 + 2,500)	3,040	
Bank charges	320	
Postage, stationery & telephone	2,910	
Carriage outwards	850	
Rent, rates and insurance	8,650	
Discounts allowed	490	
Lighting and heating	1,760	
		64,340
		38,970

(b)   (i)   *Adjustment for closing stock*

Under SSAP 2 *Disclosure of accounting policies*, costs must be *matched* against revenues in the same period. The stock will not be sold until the next accounting period, so it accords with the accruals (matching) concept that the cost of the stock should be carried forward into the next period.

SSAP 9 *Stocks and long-term contracts* states that stock should be valued at the lower of cost and net realisable value. The cost (£49,300) is lower than the net realisable value (£65,450), so it is the cost figure which should be used.

(ii)   *Bad debt*

The prudence concept (SSAP 2) states that all liabilities and losses which have arisen or are likely to arise in respect of the financial year to which the accounts relate, must be taken into account. The debt of £2,500 is not recoverable because the liquidator has stated that there are no assets available to repay creditors. The £2,500 must therefore be treated as a bad debt and be written off this year against profit.

Although the liquidation of the debtor occurred after the year end, the above still applies. Under SSAP 17 *Post balance sheet events*, this would be an adjusting event, since it provides evidence of conditions existing at the balance sheet date.

9   SANDRO VENUS

(a) JOURNAL ENTRIES

			£	£
(i)	DEBIT	Bad debt expense (5% × 18,740)	937	
	CREDIT	Provision for doubtful debts		937

Note. The bad debts written off figure (£830) has already been credited to the sales ledger control account.

			£	£
(ii)	DEBIT	Drawings	500	
	CREDIT	Purchases		500

			£	£
(iii)	DEBIT	Other debtors	3,500	
	CREDIT	Disposals		3,500
	DEBIT	Disposals	5,500	
	CREDIT	Motor vehicles: cost		5,500
	DEBIT	Motor vehicles (acc. depn.)	2,400	
	CREDIT	Motor vehicles: disposals		2,400
	DEBIT	Motor vehicles: disposals	400	
	CREDIT	Profit and loss account (profit on disposal)		400

(b) SANDRO VENUS
TRADING, PROFIT AND LOSS ACCOUNT FOR THE YEAR ENDED 31 MARCH 20X7

	£	£
Sales		187,325
Less returns inwards		(1,437)
		185,888
Cost of sales		
Opening stock	27,931	
Purchases (W)	103,151	
	131,082	
Less closing stock	(30,229)	
		(100,853)
Gross profit		85,035
Bank deposit interest		972
Profit on sale of vehicle		400
		86,407
Expenses		
Depreciation (6,084 × 1,375 × 2,780)	10,249	
Carriage outwards	657	
Rent, rates and insurance	7,721	
Bad debts (830 + 937)	1,767	
Postage and stationery	524	
Wages and NIC	29,344	
Discounts allowed	373	
Bank charges	693	
Telephone	4,307	
Lighting and heating	3,755	
Motor expenses	4,762	
Net profit		64,152
		22,255

Working: purchases

	£
Per trial balance	103,742
Plus carriage inwards	923
Less drawings	(500)
Less returns outwards	(1,014)
	103,151

Answers

(c) *Notes for telephone conversation with Sandro Venus on incorporation*

(i) *Liability of owner for debts of the business*

This can be contrasted with the liability of a sole trader. A sole trader is liable for all the debts of a business to the extent of his or her personal wealth. By contrast, a shareholder in a limited company is liable for the debts of the business only to the extent of his or her shareholding in the company.

The maximum a shareholder therefore stands to lose in the event that the company becomes unable to pay its debts is the capital in the business. On the face of it, this is a clear advantage.

In practice, with a small company such as yours, creditors, particularly bankers, often ask for personal guarantees. If the advantage is more apparent than real, you will need to consider other factors.

(ii) *Legal identity*

A limited company is a separate legal entity from its members. This would be true even if you were the only shareholder and director. As a sole trader, you are not considered to be a separate legal person from the business.

There are many consequences of this legal status. Limited liability, mentioned above, is one. Others include the fact that if you die the company is not automatically dissolved - your shareholding can pass to someone else. Assets and liabilities will be owned by the company, not by you. There are rules on distribution of capital, which must be retained to meet the company's debts.

(iii) *Regulation of the production of financial statements*

A sole trader can prepare accounts in any suitable form, although it is a good idea, for tax and record-keeping purposes, to follow best practice. By contrast, a limited company is subject to much more detailed regulation.

You will have to prepare and deliver to the Registry of Companies, annual accounts and an annual return (a summary of your situation). For many limited companies the accounts must be audited, although your turnover is well below the £350,000 threshold required for this.

The form and content of accounts are regulated in the main by company law (specifically the Companies Act, 1985). They must give a 'true and fair view' of the company's affairs. They must also, in order to give a true and fair view, conform with so-called 'accounting standards' set by the Accounting Standards Board.

10 JONATHAN BROWN

(a) There is a conflict here between the accruals or matching concept and the prudence concept. The accruals concept states that costs should be matched against revenue which they generate. Thus it might be argued that, since half the revenue expected to result from the advertising campaign will be achieved in 20X6, it might be appropriate to defer half the costs of the advertising campaign until 20X6. This would mean that £1,400 would be treated as deferred expenditure (an asset) in the financial statements for the year ended 31 December 20X5. However, the concept of prudence states that profits (and revenue) should not be anticipated but that provision should be made for all known losses (and expenses). When prudence and accruals conflict, prudence prevails. Therefore all the cost of the advertising campaign should be written off as an expense in the 20X5 accounts.

(b) When the proprietor of a business takes stock for his own use, it counts as drawings, which are a deduction from the owner's capital. The entries to record the drawings are:

DEBIT   Drawings   £500
CREDIT   Purchases   £500

(c) The receipt of compensation from the insurance company is contingent upon the outcome of the court case. As such it is a *contingent asset* and the accounting treatment is governed by FRS 12 *Provisions, contingent liabilities and contingent assests*. As the asset is only contingent, it should not be recognised in the financial statements for the year ended 31 December 20X5. If the cash inflow is 'probable' it should be disclosed in a note to the accounts. If the contingent asset is only 'possible' it should not be disclosed at all. It is not clear whether the term 'reasonable' means probable or possible and the solicitor would need to be consulted further to determine the accounting treatment.

(d) Under the business entity concept the business is a separate entity from Jonathan Brown as a person. This applies for accounting purposes, although not for legal purposes. The loan should not, therefore, be disclosed in the financial statements of the business: it is a personal transaction between Jonathan Brown and the bank.

11   LOCKE, BERKELEY AND HUME

(a) JACK, JANE, SREELA AND BHATTI
STATEMENT OF ADJUSTED PROFIT FOR THE YEAR ENDED 30 SEPTEMBER 20X8

	£'000
Profit per Jack	164,100
Bad debt written off	(12,500)
Accrual for delivery costs	(4,200)
	147,400

(b) The reason why the profit must be adjusted for the liquidation of the debtor is that, if the debtor does not pay, the business has sustained a loss. The prudence concept requires that provision must be made for all known and foreseeable losses at the earliest opportunity. Therefore the bad debt must be written off in the year ended 30 September 20X8, with a corresponding reduction in the debtors figure in the balance sheet.

The accruals concept requires that all costs must be matched against the income which they helped to generate. The invoice for delivery costs of £4,200 relates to equipment sold during the year ended 30 September 20X8, even though it was not received until after the year end. Since the sales income was recorded in the year, the delivery costs must be matched against this income and recorded in the year ended 30 September 20X8.

(c) PARTNERS' CAPITAL ACCOUNTS

	Jack £	*Jane* £	*Sreela* £	*Bhatti* £	*Jack* £	*Jane* £	*Sreela* £	*Bhatti* £
Bal b/f 1.10.X7					37,000	31,000	26,000	-
Cash 1.10.X7								50,000
Goodwill 1.10.X7	60,000	48,000	36,000	36,000	75,000	60,000	45,000	-
Bal c/f 30.9.X8	52,000	43,000	35,000	14,000				
	112,000	91,000	71,000	50,000	112,000	91,000	71,000	50,000

(d) JACK, JANE, SREELA AND BHATTI
PROFIT AND LOSS APPROPRIATION ACCOUNT
FOR THE YEAR ENDED 30 SEPTEMBER 20X8

	£	£
Adjusted net profit		147,400
Less partners' salaries		
Jack	15,000	
Jane	12,000	
Sreela	8,000	
Bhatti	8,000	
		43,000
Less interest on capital (10%)		
Jack	5,200	
Jane	4,300	
Sreela	3,500	
Bhatti	1,400	
		14,400
		90,000
Shared in profit sharing ratio:		
Jack 5/15	30,000	
Jane 4/15	24,000	
Sreela 3/15	18,000	
Bhatti 3/15	18,000	
		90,000

(e) PARTNERS' CURRENT ACCOUNTS

	Jack £	Jane £	Sreela £	Bhatti £	Jack £	Jane £	Sreela £	Bhatti £
Bal b/f 1.10.X7					5,300	4,200	3,100	-
Interest on Capital					5,200	4,300	3,500	1,400
Salaries					15,000	12,000	8,000	8,000
Drawings	48,200	39,300	29,800	25,400				
Profit					30,000	24,000	18,000	18,000
Bal c/f 30.9.X8	7,300	5,200	2,800	2,000				
	55,500	44,500	32,600	27,400	55,500	44,500	32,600	27,400

12 MIDDLEMARCH

> **Tutorial note.** Central assessments are not as time pressured as traditional examinations, but a high level of accuracy is required. You should, therefore, have got the entries right for the goodwill adjustment. If you have any doubts about this, look back to your Tutorial Text and practise some more questions.

(a) MIDDLEMARCH
APPROPRIATION ACCOUNT FOR THE YEAR ENDED 31 MARCH 20X4

	£	£
Net profit		56,740
Less interest on partner's loan		(640)
Adjusted net profit		56,100
Less partners salaries		
Lydgate	5,000	
Garth	6,000	
		11,000
Less interest on capital		
Brooke	2,300	
Featherstone	1,400	
Lydgate	900	
Garth	500	
		5,100
		40,000
Balance of profits shared		
Brooke		16,000
Featherstone		12,000
Lydgate		8,000
Garth		4,000
		40,000

(b)   PARTNERS' CAPITAL ACCOUNTS

	Brooke	Feather-stone	Lydgate	Garth		Brooke	Feather-stone	Lydgate	Garth
	£	£	£	£		£	£	£	£
Goodwill	12,000	9,000	6,000	3,000	Bal 1 April X3	20,000	14,000	9,000	-
Bal c/f	23,000	14,000	9,000	5,000	Goodwill	15,000	9,000	6,000	-
					Capital introduced	-	-	-	8,000
	35,000	23,000	15,000	8,000		35,000	23,000	15,000	8,000

PARTNERS' CURRENT ACCOUNTS

	Brooke	Feather-stone	Lydgate	Garth		Brooke	Feather-stone	Lydgate	Garth
	£	£	£	£		£	£	£	£
Bal 1 April X3	-	-	1,800	-	Bal 1 April X3	4,500	3,800	-	-
Drawings	19,320	16,100	14,300	13,600	Interest on loan	640	-	-	-
Bal c/f	4,120	1,100	-	-	Interest on capital	2,300	1,400	900	500
					Salary	-	-	5,000	6,000
					Profit share	16,000	12,000	8,000	4,000
					Bal c/f	-	-	2,200	3,100
	23,440	17,200	16,100	13,600		23,440	17,200	16,100	13,600

(c) (i) Under the prudence concept of SSAP 2 *Disclosure of accounting policies*, provision is made for all known losses in the light of the information available at the time of preparation of the accounts. If the debtor has gone into liquidation then at the time the accounts are prepared, a loss becomes known. Under SSAP 17 *Accounting for post balance sheet events*, this would be an example of an adjusting event. Even if the event occurs after the year end, it provides additional evidence of conditions existing at the balance sheet date. In this case the debt exists at the year end and the event of liquidation provides additional evidence of the collectibility of the debt. As we now know it to be irrecoverable, provision for the loss must be made in the financial statements to 31 March 20X4 and not in next year's accounts.

(ii) Under FRS 12 *Provisions, contingent liabilities and contingent assests* the legal case could be a contingent liability. This is:

'A possible obligation that arises from past events and whose existence will be confirmed only by the occurrence or non-occurrence of one or more uncertain future events not wholly within the entity's control.'

Under FRS 12 a contingent liability should never be accrued for in the accounts – if the outflow is probable, a contingent liability should be disclosed. However, in this case an outflow is unlikely, so there is no need to disclose or provide.

(iii) At the date of admission of the partner the goodwill in the firm was valued at £30,000. In the absence of any clause in the partnership in respect of goodwill then each partner will be entitled to a share of the goodwill in proportion to the profit sharing ratios. Under the old profit sharing ratios Brooke would be entitled to five-tenths of the goodwill, £15,000, Featherstone to three tenths, £9,000, and Lydgate two-tenths, £6,000. With the introduction of the new partner, although Featherstone and Lydgate retain the same profit share, Brooke's share reduces to four tenths. This would mean that her share of the goodwill would be reduced to £12,000. To compensate her for this loss, goodwill would be credited to the original partners' capital accounts in their old profit sharing ratios and then it is eliminated to all partners' capital accounts in the new profit sharing ratios. The net result of this is that Brooke's capital account is increased by £3,000, the amount of her loss as a result of the introduction of the new partner.

(iv) The balances of Lydgate and Garth at the end of the year show a debit balance. This means that they have withdrawn more money from the partnership than the credit to their accounts entitled them and disadvantages the other partners who have credit balances and who have to fund the excess. To overcome this problem the partnership agreement could be altered to give partners interest on their current accounts and/or charge interest where debit balances are outstanding at the end of the year.

13 SHIPS

(a)

PARTNERS' CURRENT ACCOUNTS

	Mary £	Nelson £	Elizabeth £		Mary £	Nelson £	Elizabeth £
Goodwill (6:4)	-	54,000	36,000	Balance b/d 1.4.X8	28,000	26,000	22,000
				Cash		40,000	
Loan account (bal. fig)	80,000		25,000	Revaluation (W)	16,000	12,000	12,000
Balance c/d 31.3.X9		51,000		Goodwill (4:3:3)	36,000	27,000	27,000
	80,000	105,000	61,000		80,000	105,000	61,000

Working: revaluation

	£'000
Valuation (328 + 26)	354
Book value (278 + 36)	314
Surplus	40

In profit sharing ratio: 4:3:3 = 16/12/12

(b) MARY, NELSON AND ELIZABETH
APPROPRIATION ACCOUNT FOR THE YEAR ENDED 3 MARCH 20X9

	£	£
Net profit		106,120
Less partners' salaries		
Mary	18,000	
Nelson	16,000	
Elizabeth	13,000	
		47,000
Less interest on capital		
Mary (28,000 × 12%)	3,360	
Nelson (26,000 × 12%)	3,120	
Elizabeth (22,000 × 12%)	2,640	
		9,120
Net profit available for appropriation		50,000
Balance of profits shared		
Mary 4/10	20,000	
Nelson 3/10	15,000	
Elizabeth 3/10	15,000	
		50,000

(c)

PARTNERS' CURRENT ACCOUNTS

	Mary £	Nelson £	Elizabeth £		Mary £	Nelson £	Elizabeth £
Drawings	38,000	30,000	29,000	Balance b/d 1.4.X8	2,500	2,160	1,870
Loan a/c (bal. fig.)	5,860			Interest on capital	3,360	3,120	2,640
Balance c/d 31.3.X9		6,280	3,510	Salaries	18,000	16,000	13,000
				Profit	20,000	15,000	15,000
	43,860	36,280	32,510		43,860	36,280	32,510

Answers

(d)

MARY: LOAN ACCOUNT

	£		£
		Capital a/c	80,000
	85,860	Current a/c	5,860
Balance c/f 31.3.X9	85,860		85,860

(e)

A Technician
ABC Accountants
5 Debit Street
Crediton

3 April 20X9

The Partners
Ships & Co
6 Credit Street
Crediton

Adjustments on Retirement of a Partner

In the partners' capital accounts I have made two adjustments to reflect Mary's retirement: goodwill and revaluation.

Goodwill

Goodwill can be defined as the excess of the fair market value of the price paid for a business over the fair market value of the individual assets and liabilities acquired. Alternatively it may be generated internally, as here. It is dependent on a wide variety of factors such as business location, reputation, staff personalities and the ability to earn profits. In the case of Ships & Co, goodwill is a genuine asset of the business with a value which would be obtained if the business were sold. In order to give the retiring partner, Mary, her fair share of all the net assets of the business, she must be given her share of the asset of goodwill. Hence the capital accounts are credited with goodwill in the old profit sharing ratio, which includes Mary. However, because goodwill is not to remain in the books of the partnership, it is necessary to remove it by debiting the capital accounts in the new profit sharing ratio.

Revaluation

The net gain on the revaluation of fixed assets is £40,000. Because the increase in value took place *before* Mary's retirement on 31 March 20X9, it makes sense to attribute it to the partners in their old profit sharing ratio of 4:3:3. Thus the capital accounts will be credited in this ratio. If this gain were not credited to Mary, the remaining partners would benefit from the net increase in value of the assets when the assets were sold. This would not be fair to the retiring partner, as the increase occurred before her retirement.

Because the new valuation is to remain in the books of the partnership, there is no need to remove it, as I did with the goodwill.

I hope this clarifies the matter for you.

Yours sincerely

A Technician

14 ALICE, BONNY AND CLYDE

> **Tutorial note**. Because interest is calculated on the year-end balance of capital, it is necessary to prepare the capital accounts in Part (b) before you can complete the appropriation account in Part (a).

(a) ALICE, BONNY AND CLYDE

APPROPRIATION ACCOUNT FOR THE YEAR ENDED 31 OCTOBER 20X4

	£	£
Profit available for appropriation		78,000
Less salaries: Alice	10,000	
Clyde	5,000	
		(15,000)
Less interest on capital		
Alice: 19,000 × 10%	1,900	
Bonny: 10,000 × 10%	1,000	
Clyde: 5,000 × 10%	500	
		(3,400)
Balance of net profit		59,600
Alice 3/6	29,800	
Bonny 2/6	19,867	
Clyde 1/6	9,933	
		59,600

(b)

CAPITAL ACCOUNTS

	Alice £	Bonny £	Clyde £		Alice £	Bonny £	Clyde £
Goodwill	15,000	10,000	5,000	Balance b/f	14,000	10,000	-
Balance c/f	19,000	10,000	5,000	Bank	-	-	10,000
				Goodwill	20,000	10,000	-
	34,000	20,000	10,000		34,000	20,000	10,000

CURRENT ACCOUNTS

	Alice £	Bonny £	Clyde £		Alice £	Bonny £	Clyde £
Drawings	38,000	19,500	15,000	Balance b/f	4,000	2,500	-
Balance c/f	7,700	3,867	433	Salary	10,000	-	5,000
				Interest on capital	1,900	1,000	500
				Profit	29,800	19,867	9,933
	45,700	23,367	15,433		45,700	23,367	15,433

15 COLERIDGE

(a)

PARTNERS' CAPITAL ACCOUNTS

	Wordsworth £'000	Quincey £'000	Southey £'000	Taylor £'000		Wordsworth £'000	Quincey £'000	Southey £'000	Taylor £'000
Goodwill (4:3:3)		20	15	15	Balance b/d	138	65	84	
Loan	213				Revaluation (5:3:2)	50	30	20	
Balance c/d		90	99	65	Goodwill (5:3:2)	25	15	10	80
					Cash				
	213	110	114	80		213	110	114	80

(b) (i) Goodwill, whether originally purchased (being defined as 'the excess of the fair market value of the price paid for a business over the fair market value of the individual assets and liabilities acquired') or whether internally generated, is dependent on a wide variety of factors such as business location, reputation, staff personalities and the ability to earn profits or 'super profits'. In the case of Coleridge & Co, goodwill is a genuine asset of the business with a value which could be obtained if the business was sold. In order to give the retiring partner his share of all the net assets of the business he must be given his share of the asset of goodwill. Hence his capital account is credited with the value of this share.

(ii) The advantages of operating as a partnership rather than as a sole trader are practical rather than legal. They include the following.

(1) Risks are spread across a larger number of people.

(2) The trader will have access to a wider network of contacts through the other partners.

(3) Partners should bring to the business not only capital but skills and experience.

(4) It may well be easier to raise finance from external sources such as banks.

(5) Economies of scale may be available, eg secretarial help.

(*Note*. You were asked for *two* examples only.)

16   STOOGE

> **Tutorial note**. Because we cannot calculate the interest on capital until we have done the capital accounts in Part (b) it makes sense to set out the proformas first, to do part (a) as far as possible, then do part (b) and finally finish off part (a).

(a)   STOOGE & CO
PROFIT AND LOSS APPROPRIATION ACCOUNT
FOR THE YEAR ENDED 31 MARCH 20X6

		£	£
Balance of net profit per ETB			80,000
Less interest on capital:	Curly	4,600	
(see Tutorial Note)	Larry	2,600	
	Mo	2,800	
			10,000
Balance of profit for appropriation			70,000
Profit share:	Curly		
	Larry	35,000	
	Mo	21,000	
		14,000	
			70,000

(b)

PARTNERS' CAPITAL ACCOUNTS

	C	L	M		C	L	M
	£	£	£		£	£	£
Goodwill 5:3:2	30,000	18,000	12,000	Balance per ETB	40,000	20,000	40,000
Balance c/d	46,000	26,000	28,000	Goodwill 6:4	36,000	24,000	–
	76,000	44,000	40,000		76,000	44,000	40,000

PARTNERS' CURRENT ACCOUNTS

	C	L	M		C	L	M
	£	£	£		£	£	£
Balance per ETB		4,000		Balance per ETB	6,000		
Drawings	30,000	24,000	32,000	Salary	30,000	20,000	20,000
Balance c/d	45,600	15,600	4,800	Interest on capital @ 10%	4,600	2,600	2,800
				Profit share	35,000	21,000	14,000
	75,600	43,600	36,800		75,600	43,600	36,800

17   PRIDE

(a)   PRIDE AND CO
APPROPRIATION ACCOUNT
FOR THE YEAR ENDED 31 OCTOBER 20X6

	£	£
Net profit		90,000
Less interest on loan		1,000
Adjusted net profit		89,000
Less partner's salaries		
Jane	15,000	
Elizabeth	10,000	
Lydia	5,000	
		30,000
Less interest on capital		
Jane: 8% × 25,000	2,000	
Elizabeth: 8% × 22,000	1,760	
Lydia: 8% × 3,000	240	
		4,000
		55,000
Balance of net profit		
Jane: ⁵⁄₁₀	27,500	
Elizabeth: ³⁄₁₀	16,500	
Lydia: ²⁄₁₀	11,000	
		55,000

(b)

To: The Partners, Pride and Co
From: A Technician   Date: 6 November 20X6

Admission of Asmah to partnership

(i)   Further to your queries with regard to the admission of Asmah, I have performed an analysis using profitability ratios. These are set out below.

	Pride and Co	*Asmah*	*Combined*
Gross profit %	$\frac{240}{600} = 40\%$	$\frac{90}{200} = 45\%$	$\frac{240+90}{600+200} = \frac{330}{800} = 41\%$
Net profit %	$\frac{90}{600} = 15\%$	$\frac{20}{200} = 10\%$	$\frac{90+20}{600+200} = \frac{110}{800} = 14\%$
Expenses/sales	$\frac{150}{600} = 25\%$	$\frac{70}{200} = 35\%$	$\frac{150+70}{600+200} = \frac{220}{800} = 28\%$

The above table shows that, if Asmah were admitted, the new partnership would benefit from an increase in gross profit percentage. Asmah's is higher, so the combination would bring the partnership's up higher. However, because Asmah's expenses are proportionally greater (35% of sales as against 25%) the combined firm would suffer from a relative increase in expenses, leading to a smaller net profit percentage.

However, it is still possible that the merger will be a good thing for Pride and Co. After all, net profit will increase in absolute terms. Furthermore a larger business may be able to achieve economies of scale, thus reducing expenses and increasing profitability.

(ii) Any changes in the constitution of a partnership, such as the admission of a new partner, require a new partnership agreement. Legally, the old partnership is dissolved and a new partnership created. The partnership agreement should deal with the following points.

(1) The new profit-sharing ratio
(2) Capital to the contributed by each partner
(3) Interest on capital
(4) Salaries, if any, to be paid to each partner. These have yet to be decided

(iii) The following adjustments would have to be made to the capital accounts of the partnership if the admission goes ahead.

PARTNERS' CAPITAL ACCOUNTS

	Jane £'000	Elizabeth £'000	Lydia £'000	Asmah £'000		Jane £'000	Elizabeth £'000	Lydia £'000	Asmah £'000
Goodwill	25	15	10	10	Balance b/d	25	22	3	
Balance c/d	50	37	13	25	Revaluation	20	12	8	
					Goodwill	30	18	12	
					Net assets				35
	75	52	23	35		75	52	23	35

18 GRACES

(a)

PARTNERS' CAPITAL ACCOUNTS

	Alice £	Ethel £	Isabella £	Flora £		Alice £	Ethel £	Isabella £	Flora £
Revaluation: motor vehicle (24 – 8.4) – 6	4,000	3,200	2,400		Balance b/f	55,000	45,000	40,000	
					Bank				30,000
Balance c/f 1.6.97	146,000	117,800	94,600	30,000	Revaluation: Land and Buildings	35,000	28,000	21,000	
					Goodwill	60,000	48,000	36,000	
	150,000	121,000	97,000	30,000		150,000	121,000	97,000	30,000

(b) *Notes for meeting*

When a new partner is admitted, the old partners rightly wish to ensure that they receive their full entitlement to partnership profits up to the date of the admission. This is the case not just for ordinary trading profits but also for unrealised gains, for example on fixed assets. It is, therefore, right that fixed assets such as land and buildings should be revalued, otherwise the new partner, Flora, would make a gain which she had not 'earned' by contributing capital or profits in her own right.

Similarly, the new partner should not have to bear any losses which arose before he or she was admitted. This includes diminutions in the value of fixed assets as well as trading losses. Thus the fall in the value of the motor vehicles is reflected in the old partners' capital accounts.

19   AMANDA BLAKE

(a)   CAPITAL ACCOUNTS

	Amanda £	John £	Sheila £	Fred £		Amanda £	John £	Sheila £	Fred £
Bal b/d 1.1.97						36,600	31,200	25,200	-
Goodwill	52,000	39,000	39,000	26,000		62,400	46,800	46,800	-
Cash									45,000
Bal c/d 31.12.97	47,000	39,000	33,000	19,000					
	99,000	78,000	72,000	45,000		99,000	78,000	72,000	45,000

(b)   APPROPRIATION ACCOUNTS FOR THE YEAR ENDED
      31 DECEMBER 1997

	£	£
Net profit per accounts		151,800
Less partners' salaries		
Amanda	14,000	
John	11,000	
Sheila	9,000	
Fred	8,000	
		(42,000)
Less interest on capital		
Amanda (10% × 47,000)	4,700	
John (10% × 39,000)	3,900	
Sheila (10% × 33,000)	3,300	
Fred	1,900	
		(13,800)
Profit available for appropriation		96,000
Profit share		
Amanda	4/12	32,000
John	3/12	24,000
Sheila	3/12	24,000
Fred	2/12	16,000
		96,000

(c)   CURRENT ACCOUNTS

	Amanda £	John £	Sheila £	Fred £		Amanda £	John £	Sheila £	Fred £
Bal b/d 1.1.97						4,200	3,600	2,700	
Interest on capital						4,700	3,900	3,300	1,900
Salaries						14,000	11,000	9,000	8,000
Drawings	51,000	38,000	36,000	24,000					
Profit						32,000	24,000	24,000	16,000
Bal c/d 31.12.97									
	54,900	42,500	39,000	25,900		54,900	42,500	39,000	25,900

20 BLUTHER

> **Tutorial note**. In Parts (a) to (c), be careful with the interest on the loan and don't forget the drawings. In answering Part (d), remember that the partners are not accountants – make your language as explicit as possible.

(a)

CAPITAL ACCOUNTS

		Bothina £	Luther £	Edwina £			Bothina £	Luther £	Edwina £
1.4.X7	Goodwill	20,000	20,000	10,000	1.4.X7	Bal b/f	20,000	15,000	
31.3.X8	Bal c/f	25,000	20,000	10,000	1.4.X7	Cash			20,000
					1.4.X7	Goodwill	25,000	25,000	
		45,000	40,000	20,000			45,000	40,000	20,000

(b) BLUTHER AND CO
PROFIT AND LOSS APPROPRIATION ACCOUNT
FOR THE YEAR ENDED 31 MARCH 20X8

		£	£
Net profit			75,500
Less interest on loan			(1,200)
Profit available for appropriation			74,300
Less interest on capital:	Bothina	2,500	
	Luther	2,000	
	Edwina	1,000	
			(5,500)
Less salaries:	Bothina	8,000	
	Edwina	5,000	
			(13,000)
Profit available for profit sharing ratio			55,800
Profit sharing ratio:	Bothina	22,320	
	Luther	22,320	
	Edwina	11,160	
			55,800

(c)

CURRENT ACCOUNTS

		Bothina £	Luther £	Edwina £			Bothina £	Luther £	Edwina £
31.3.X8	Drawings	10,000	12,000	8,000	1.4.X7	Bal b/f	5,000	3,000	
31.3.X8	Bal c/f	27,820	16,520	9,160	31.3.X8	Interest on loan		1,200	
					31.3.X8	Interest on capital	2,500	2,000	1,000
					31.3.X8	Salaries	8,000		5,000
					31.3.X8	Profit	22,320	22,320	11,160
		37,820	28,520	17,160			37,820	28,520	17,160

(d)

MEMO

To: Partners, Bluther & Co
From: A Technician
Date: 20 May 20X8

Queries on accounts for the year ended 31 March 20X8

(i)   Although the liquidation of the debtor took place after the year end, it affects the debtors position for Bluther & Co at the year end. In other words, the debtors in the balance sheet as at 31.3.X8 are not as originally thought.

This type of occurrence is governed by an accounting standard, SSAP 17 *Accounting for post balance sheet events*. The standard defines post balance sheet events as those events occurring after the balance sheet date which provide additional evidence of conditions existing at the balance sheet date. The accounts must be adjusted by writing off the bad debt.

(ii) Goodwill is the difference between the value of a business as a whole (or the price paid for a business), and the aggregate of the fair values of its separable net assets.

The usual treatment of goodwill (in this case £50,000) arising on the admission of a new partner is to credit it to the partners' capital accounts in the *old* profit sharing ratio. This reflects the fact that it is the old partners who have earned the goodwill. Thus the capital accounts of Bothina and Luther are each credited with £25,000.

Generally, goodwill, being a subjective figure, does not remain in the books. The amount is taken out of the books by debiting the partners in the *new* profit sharing ratio. The accounts of the partners would be debited as follows.

	£
Bothina	20,000
Luther	20,000
Edwina	10,000

The contribution of Bothina and Luther is reflected in the £5,000 credit in their capital accounts. From now on, any goodwill built up by the partnership will be shared according to the new profit-sharing ratio, since Edwina will also have contributed.

(iii) When a new partner is admitted, the old partners rightly wish to ensure that they receive their full entitlement to partnership profits up to the date of the admission. This is the case not just for ordinary trading profits but also for unrealised gains, for example on fixed assets. It is, therefore, fight that fixed assets such as land and buildings should be revalued, otherwise the new partner, Edwina would benefit from a gain, or bear a loss, which she had not 'earned'.

21 FINALISE

> **Tutorial note**. Admission of a new partner comes up very regularly. You need to know how to deal with the goodwill and the new profit sharing ratio. Other tricky points here include the interest on the loan and on the drawings and capital.

(a) CAPITAL ACCOUNTS

		Thomas	*Gina*	*Henry*	*Alex*			*Thomas*	*Gina*	*Henry*	*Alex*
		£	£	£	£			£	£	£	£
1.10.X7	Goodwill	20,000	20,000	20,000	20,000	1.10.X7	Bal b/f	10,000	15,000	12,000	-
30.9.X8	Bal c/f	22,000	27,000	8,000	5,000	1.10.X7	Cash	-	-	-	25,000
						1.10.X7	Goodwill	32,000	32,000	16,000	-
		42,000	47,000	28,000	25,000			42,000	47,000	28,000	25,000

(b) THOMAS, GINA, HENRY AND ALEX
PROFIT AND LOSS APPROPIRATION ACCOUNT
FOR THE YEAR ENDED 30 SEPTEMBER 20X8

		£	£
Net profit			56,000
Less interest on loan			(600)
Profit available for appropriation			55,400
Plus interest on drawings:	Thomas	1,200	
	Gina	1,100	
	Henry	1,300	
	Alex	1,000	
			4,600
Less interest on capital:	Thomas	2,200	
	Gina	2,700	
	Henry	800	
	Alex	500	
			(6,200)
Less salaries	Thomas	7,000	
	Henry	5,000	
			(12,000)
Profit available for profit sharing ratio			41,800
Profit sharing ratio:	Thomas	10,450	
	Gina	10,450	
	Henry	10,450	
	Alex	10,450	
			(41,800)

(c) CURRENT ACCOUNTS

		Thomas £	Gina £	Henry £	Alex £			Thomas £	Gina £	Henry £	Alex £
30.9.X8	Drawings	12,000	11,000	13,000	10,000	1.10.X7	Bal b/f	2,000	4,000	1,000	
30.9.X8	Interest on					30.9.X8	Interest				
	drawings	1,200	1,100	1,300	1,000		on loan			600	
30.9.X8	Bal c/f	8,450	5,050	3,550		30.9.X8	Interest on				
							capital	2,200	2,700	800	500
						30.9.X8	Salaries	7,000		5,000	
						30.8.X8	Profit	10,450	10,450	10,450	10,450
						30.8.X8	Bal c/f				50
		21,650	17,150	17,850	11,000			21,650	17,150	17,850	11,000

(d)

MEMO

To: Partners
From: A Technician
Date: 20 November 20X8

Accounting queries

(i)   *Stock valuation*

The rule for valuation of stock follows the prudence concept. It is set out in SSAP 9 *Stocks and long-term contracts*, which states that stock should be valued at the lower of cost and net realisable value.

The thinking behind this rule is that we should not anticipate profit. The partnership should, therefore, continue to value the stock items at £10 each.

(ii) *Liability of partnership and limited company*

The liability of a partnership is *unlimited*. This means that, should the partnership go bankrupt, the personal assets of the partners could be used to pay off the partnership's debts.

By, contrast, the liability of shareholders of a limited company is limited to the amount unpaid on the shares. In the case of a company limited by guarantee, the members' liability is limited to the amount guaranteed.

22   PRACTICE QUESTION: DEPRECIATION

(a) Where fixed assets are disposed of for an amount which is greater or less than their book value, the surplus or deficiency should be reflected in the results of the year and disclosed separately if material. Following the provisions of FRS 3 *Reporting financial performance,* a material amount should be disclosed on the face of the profit and loss account.

(b) A change from one method of providing depreciation to another is permissible only on the grounds that the new method will give a fairer presentation of the results and of the financial position. In these circumstances the unamortised cost of the asset should be written off over the remaining useful life on the new basis commencing with the period in which the change is made. The effect should be disclosed in the year of change, if material.

23   PRACTICE QUESTION: STOCKS

(a) *Cost* is that expenditure which has been incurred in the normal course of business in bringing the product or service to its present location and condition. This expenditure should include:

(i) cost of purchase (including import duties, transport and handling costs and any other directly attributable costs, less trade discounts, rebates and subsidies);

(ii) any costs of conversion appropriate to that location and condition (including direct labour and expenses, and attributable production overheads).

(b) *Net realisable value* is the actual or estimated selling price (net of trade but before settlement discounts) less:

(i) all further costs to completion; and
(ii) all costs to be incurred in marketing, selling and distributing.

24   SSAP 13

Tutorial note. Parts (a) and (b) here are straightforward. However, part (c) may have caused candidates problems. If a question involves a SSAP or FRS, you will almost certainly be required to demonstrate understanding as well as rote learning.

(a) SSAP 13 recognises three categories of research and development expenditure.

(i) *Pure or basic research* is directed primarily towards the advancement of knowledge.

(ii) *Applied research* is directed towards exploiting pure research, for a specific aim or objective, other than work defined as development.

(iii) *Development expenditure* is directed towards the introduction or improvement of specific products or processes.

(b) Only development expenditure may be capitalised and then only if it satisfies all of the following conditions:

(i) there is a clearly defined project;

(ii) the relevant expenditure is clearly and separately identifiable;

(iii) the project is considered to be technically, environmentally and commercially feasible;

(iv) the expenditure (including any future expenditure) is expected to be more than recoverable from the future revenues that will flow from the project;

(v) adequate physical and human resources exist to complete the project;

(vi) management has made a decision to allocate the necessary resources to the project.

(c) The need for the standard arose from a concern that some companies were capitalising large amounts of R&D that were unlikely to be recovered from future revenues. This practice inflated the net assets of companies who followed it and made it difficult to compare their accounts with those of companies that wrote off their R&D expenditure. Equally, other companies were writing off large amounts of expenditure which could have been deferred. The standard thus imposed consistency and comparability.

The particular case that it is thought may have prompted the ASC to act was that of Rolls-Royce who went bankrupt and had to be nationalised at a time when it was carrying very large sums in its balance sheet in respect of capitalised R&D costs for the RB 211 aero engine.

25   FUN

(a) The journal entries required are as follows.

	Debit £'000	Credit £'000
Dividends (p&l) (£8,000,000 × 0.1)	800	
Dividends payable		800
Corporation tax (p&l)	972	
Corporation tax (creditor)		972
Interest charge (p&l) (8% × £3,600,000 × 1/12)	24	
Accruals		24

(b) FUN LIMITED
PROFIT AND LOSS ACCOUNT FOR THE YEAR ENDED 31 SEPTEMBER 20X8

	£'000
Turnover (continuing operations) (W1)	14,363
Cost of sales (W2)	6,464
Gross profit	7,899
Distribution costs	2,669
Administrative expenses	2,042
Operating profit (continuing operations)	3,188
Interest payable and similar charges (300+24)	324
Profit on ordinary activities before taxation	2,864
Tax on profit on ordinary activities	972
Profit on ordinary activities after taxation	1,892
Dividends (480+800)	1,280
Retained profit for the financial year	612

Workings

1   *Turnover*

	£'000
Sales	14,595
Returns inwards	(232)
	14,363

2   *Cost of sales*

	£'000
Opening stock	1,893
Purchases	6,671
Carriage inwards	87
Returns outwards	(146)
Closing stock	(2,041)
	6,464

(b) NOTES FOR BOARD MEETING DEALING WITH ACCOUNTING MATTERS

(i)   A share premium arises when a company sells shares for a price which is higher than the nominal value. By 'premium' is meant the difference between the issue price of the share and its nominal value. For example, if a share with a nominal value of £1 was issued for £1.20, then the accounting entries would be:

DEBIT	Cash	£1.20	
CREDIT	Share capital		£1.00
CREDIT	Share premium		£0.20

The revaluation reserve arose because at some point an asset was revalued. The balance represents the excess of the fair value of the asset over its net value. For example, if the asset had a net book value of £600,000, and its market value was £950,000, the accounting entries would be:

DEBIT	Fixed asset	£350,000	
CREDIT	Revaluation reserve		£350,000

(ii) It is by no means certain that a leased asset can be kept off the balance sheet. The accounting treatment of leased assets is governed by SSAP 21 *Accounting for leases and hire purchase contracts*.

The correct treatment depends on whether the lease is a finance lease or an operating lease. SSAP 21 defines a finance lease as a lease which transfers substantially all the risks and rewards of ownership of an asset to the lessee. An operating lease is a lease other than a finance lease.

If the lease is a finance lease, it should be recorded in Fun Ltd's balance sheet as a asset and as an obligation to pay future rentals. The amount recorded should be the present value of the minimum lease payments derived by discounting them at the interest rate implicit in the lease.

If, however, the lease is an operating lease, the asset belongs to the lessor, and so is not shown on the balance sheet of Fun Ltd. Rentals are charged to the profit and loss account, but future rentals are not shown as a liability on the balance sheet of Fun Ltd.

26 WOODPECKER

> **Tutorial note**. A tricky feature of this question is the share capital and reserves. Study our suggested solution carefully.

				£'000	£'000
(a)	(i)	DEBIT Ordinary share capital		400	
		CREDIT Share premium,			400

Being correction of error in crediting proceeds of share issue to ordinary share capital (800,000 shares @ 50p premium each = £400,000)

	(ii)	DEBIT Share premium		10	
		CREDIT Ordinary Share capital			100

Representing bonus share issue (2,400,000 ordinary shares in issue at the year end; 1 for 6 issue ie 400,000 ordinary shares of 25p each; reserves used in order: capital redemption reserve, share premium, other reserves)

	(iii)	DEBIT Preference share dividend		15	
		CREDIT Preference share dividend payable			15

Being final preference dividend (10% × £300,000 shares = £30,000 less interim dividend paid £15,000)

	(iv)	DEBIT Interest charge		36	
		CREDIT Accruals			36

Being interest on debentures payable (8% debentures of £450,000 = £36,000)

	(v)	DEBIT Investment revaluation reserve		150	
		DEBIT Amounts written off investments (P & L)		50	
		CREDIT Investment property			200

Being write-down of investment property to valuation (as there is an insufficient balance in the investment revaluation reserve the remaining £50,000 is written off to the P & L)

	(vi)	DEBIT Audit fees		25	
		CREDIT Accruals			25

Being accrual for audit fees

	(vii)	DEBIT Taxation charge		275	
		CREDIT Taxation payable			275

Being taxation charge for the year

				£'000	£'000
	(viii)	DEBIT Amortisation of goodwill		5	
		CREDIT Goodwill			5

Being amortisation of goodwill for the year (£500,000 divided by ten years = £5,000)

(b) WOODPECKER LIMITED
PROFIT AND LOSS ACCOUNT FOR THE YEAR ENDED 31 MARCH 20X4

(i)

	Note	£000s
Turnover		
Continuing operations		8,086
Cost of sales		4,829
Gross profit		3,257
Distribution costs		1,751
Administrative expenses		631
Operating profit		
Continuing operations		875
Amounts written off investments		50
Amortisation of goodwill		5
Interest payable and similar charges		36
Profit on ordinary activities before taxation		784
Tax on profit on ordinary activities		275
Profit on ordinary activities after taxation		509
Dividends		30
Retained profit for the financial year		479

WOODPECKER LIMITED
BALANCE SHEET AS AT 31 MARCH 20X4

	Note	£'000	£'000
Fixed assets			
Intangible assets		15	
Tangible assets		1,963	
Investment property		600	
			2,578
Current assets			
Stocks		937	
Debtors		842	
Cash at bank and in hand		3	
		1,782	
Creditors: amounts falling due within one year		1,103	
Net current assets (liabilities)			679
Total assets less current liabilities			3,257
Creditors: amounts falling due after more than one year			450
			2,807
Capital and reserves			
Called up share capital			1,000
Share premium			550
Profit and loss account			1,257
			2,807

Workings

		£'000
1	*Cost of sales*	
	Opening stock	731
	Purchases	5,035
		5,766
	Less closing stock	(937)
		4,829

2   *Allocation of expenses*

	Distribution costs £'000	Administrative expenses £'000
Advertising	56	-
Salaries and wages (75/25)	1,004	335
Increase in provision for doubtful debts	-	17
Salesmen's commission	106	-
Motor expenses	47	31
Light & heat	20	6
Insurance	29	9
Audit	-	25
General expenses	186	48
Directors' remuneration	49	102
Depreciation: motor vehicles	151	38
Depreciation: fixtures and fittings	65	-
Depreciation: office equipment	22	15
Depreciation: buildings	16	5
	1,751	631

3   *Dividend*

	£'000
Interim preference dividend	15
Final preference dividend proposed	15
	30

4   *Fixed assets*

	Cost £'000	Acc.depn. £'000	Net book value £'000
Land and buildings	1,267	138	1,129
Fixtures and fittings	632	241	391
Motor vehicles	745	408	337
Office equipment	194	88	106
	2,838	875	1,963

5   *Debtors*

	£'000	£'000
Trade debtors	840	
Less provision for doubtful debts	37	
Prepayment		803
		39
		842

6   *Creditors: amounts falling due within one year*

	£'000
Bank overdraft	139
Trade creditors	568
Corporation tax payable	275
Dividends payable	15
Accruals	106
	1,103

7   *Called up share capital*

	£'000
Issued, allotted and fully paid is:	
2,800,000 ordinary shares of 25p	700
300,000 10% preference shares of £1	300
	1,000

8   *Profit and loss account*   £'000

At 1 April 20X4   778
Retained profit for the year   479
                                                                  1,257

(ii)

(1)   *Share capital*
Authorised share capital is   £
4,000,000 10% preference shares of £1   1,000,000
500,000 10% preference shares of £1   500,000
                                                             1,500,000

Issued, allotted and fully paid: £
    2,800,000 ordinary shares of 25p   700,000
    300,000 10% preference shares of   300,000
£1

                                                             1,000,000

(2)   *Directors' remuneration*
The amounts paid to directors were   £
Fees as directors   7,000
Other emoluments (including pension contributions)   144,000

Emoluments of the chairman (excluding pension contributions) amounted to £33,000. The emoluments of the highest paid director amounted to £59,000 (excluding pension contributions). Other directors emoluments were within the following range:

£40,000 – £45,000: 1

(c)   Goodwill, as defined by FRS 10, is the difference between the value and liabilities of a business as a whole and the aggregate of the fair values of its separable assets.

27   TINY TOYS

(a)

		£	£
(i)	DEBIT Audit fees	950	
	CREDIT Accruals		950

Being provision for audit fees

(ii)	DEBIT Share premium account	7,500	
	CREDIT Ordinary share capital		7,500

Being a bonus issue of ordinary shares

(iii)	DEBIT Suspense account	150	
	CREDIT Accruals (motor expenses)		150

Being correction of a misposting for motor expenses not yet billed

(iv)	DEBIT Suspense account	5,000	
	CREDIT Profit and loss account		5,000

Being the profit made on the sale of a building, incorrectly posted to the suspense account

(v)	DEBIT Interest payable	100	
	CREDIT Creditors		100

Being the accrual of one month's interest on the 12% debentures

(b)   TINY TOYS LIMITED
PROFIT AND LOSS ACCOUNT FOR THE YEAR ENDED 31 DECEMBER 20X3

	£	£
Turnover		
Continuing operations		183,500
Cost of sales		114,200
Gross profit		69,300
Administrative costs	49,185	
Distribution costs	52,935	
		102,120
Operating loss		
Continuing operations		32,820
Profit on sale of fixed asset		5,000
Loss on ordinary activities before interest		27,820
Interest payable and similar charges		100
Loss on ordinary activities for the financial year		27,920

TINY TOYS LIMITED
BALANCE SHEET AS AT 31 DECEMBER 20X3

	£	£
Fixed assets		
Tangible assets		40,500
Current assets		
Stocks	12,900	
Debtors	37,230	
Cash in hand and at bank	4,500	
	54,630	
Current liabilities		
Creditors: amounts falling due within one year	18,350	
Net current assets		36,280
Total assets less current liabilities		76,780
Creditors: amount falling due after more than one year		
Debentures		10,000
		66,780

	£
Capital and reserves	
Called up share capital	32,500
Share premium	7,500
Profit and loss account	26,780
	66,780

Workings

		£
1	*Cost of sales*	
	Opening stock	12,800
	Purchases	114,300
	Closing stock	(12,900)
		114,200

2   *Profit on sale of fixed assets*

NBV £32,500, proceeds £37,500, therefore profit £5,000

3 *Administrative and distribution expenses*

	Administrative £	Distribution £
Audit fee	950	
Rates (3,900 – 330 = 3,570)	1,785	1,785
Bad debt	1,000	
Provision for doubtful debts	200	
Light and heat	1,000	850
Carriage outwards		3,100
Motor expenses	750	6,000
Advertising		2,200
Directors' salaries	25,000	20,000
Salesmen's commission		5,000
Salaries		
(£75,000 – 45,000 – 5,000)	15,000	10,000
Vehicles depreciation	500	2,000
Buildings depreciation	2,000	2,000
Office equipment depreciation	500	
General expenses	500	
Total	49,185	52,935

4 *Tangible assets*

	Cost £	Acc. depn. £	NBV £
Premises	40,000	12,000	28,000
Equipment	4,000	1,500	2,500
Vehicles	20,000	10,000	10,000
	64,000	23,500	40,500

5 *Debtors*

	£
Debtors	38,900
Less provision	2,000
Plus prepayments	330
	37,230

6 *Creditors*

		£
Creditors		17,000
Accruals		
Audit fee	950	
Light and hear	150	
Motor expenses	150	
Interest	100	
		1,350
Total		18,350

7 *Called up share capital and reserves*

	£	£
Ordinary share capital (25,000 + 7,500)		32,500
Share premium account (15,000 – 7,500)		7,500
Profit and loss account		
Brought forward	54,700	
Loss for year	(27,920)	
Carried forward		26,780
Total		66,780

(c)

Tutorial note. The following solution gives an example of an approach to this question. Where interpretation is required credit is given for all relevant points made. The inclusion of ratios is not necessary; candidates may score equally well from discussion made without ratios.

(i)   *Working Capital*

Working capital is the total current assets less total current liabilities ie net current assets. The control of working capital is vital to the business being able to continue. For example if debtor control is weak payment may be late (or not forthcoming) and the company will not have the resources to pay its own suppliers.

Liquidity may be measured by the use of ratio analysis.

The acid test or 'quick ratio' compares current assets (less stock) to current liabilities.

Tiny Toys' acid test = £54,630 – 12,900/18,350 = 2.3 times

This seems reasonable, although without comparative figures (previous years, industry averages) it is difficult to comment. It is important to break down the analysis of working capital into its components.

$$\text{Stock turnover} = \frac{\text{Cost of sales}}{\text{Average stock}} = \frac{£114,200}{£12,850} = 8.9 \text{ times}$$

$$\text{Debtor days} = \frac{\text{Debtors}}{\text{Sales per day}} = \frac{38,900}{183,500} \times 365 = 77 \text{ days}$$

$$\text{Creditor days} = \frac{\text{Creditors}}{\text{Cost of sales per day}} = \frac{17,000}{114,200} \times 365 = 54 \text{ days}$$

Stock turnover appears high. Although keeping a tight control on stocks is good working capital management, sufficient stock must be held to avoid loss of sales due to items being out of stock. Stock levels are relatively low and this should be investigated.

Debtor days also seems quite high, especially compared to creditor days. The former should be more tightly controlled, whilst the latter should be extended, although not at the expense of lost prompt payment discounts.

Considering that Tiny Toys have sold an asset for cash for £37,500 during the year, and just made a debenture issue for £10,000 the balance of cash appears small. The actual amount is reasonable for the size of company, but it is worrying that it has achieved this balance through a fixed asset sale and debenture issue, rather than operating activities. The company cannot continue to sell its assets (assuming they are saleable) without adversely affecting its operating performance and cash balance. For example, if the space supplied by the building which has just been sold is still needed, a similar amount of space will need to be rented. Rent will require cash payments and will also appear as an expense in the profit and loss account.

With respect to the balance currently held at the bank, interest bearing accounts should be investigated.

(ii) *Profitability*

Tiny Toys has made a very large net loss, reducing its brought forward balance of reserves by approximately half. Again trends need to be considered (within the company, the industry and the economy). However, the gross profit margin is 38%. Since this becomes a loss after expenses, further investigation is obviously critical.

Sales levels and mix and sales prices should be compared to previous years and industry averages. The costs of the company also need to be investigated. For example, are all staff being fully employed, could premises be rented rather than owned, are all vehicles required for business purposes? The size of directors' emoluments relative to the results of the company should also be considered. The size of the loss makes the questions extremely urgent and finding solutions may well be critical to the survival of the company.

(iii)   *Profit and cash*

The profit and loss account and the balance sheet are prepared on the accruals concept. The accruals concept is defined in SSAP 2 as the matching of costs against those revenues they help to produce, and the matching of income and charges to the financial period in which they occur (as opposed to when they are received/paid).

The profit figure is therefore based on the accruals concept. However it is also important to consider cash. A high profit figure does not necessarily mean large cash receipts, for example a company may have a poor credit control system whereby debtors delay payment for considerable periods. A company needs cash to pay suppliers, to produce its products or provide a service; if cash is not received it will be unable to pay for supplies and therefore unable to continue to supply its own products/service. It is therefore vital to understand the difference between profit and cash and ensure sufficient cash is available to generate profit.

(d) SSAP 2 defines an accounting policy as the specific accounting bases selected and consistently followed by a business enterprise as being, in the opinion of its management, appropriate to its circumstances and best suited to present fairly its results and financial position.

An accounting base is a method developed for applying fundamental accounting concepts (ie going concern, consistency, prudence, accruals) to financial transactions. More than one recognised accounting base may exist for dealing with particular items.

As there may be a range of accounting bases available to a company, users need to know the base used in order to be able to understand the figures presented in the financial statements. For this reason the accounting policy note to the accounts is extremely important.

(i)   *Depreciation* (required by FRS 15 *Tangible fixed assets*) spreads the net cost of a fixed asset over its useful economic life, in line with the accruals concept. However, there are many bases on which this may be done, for example straight line or reducing balance. The base selected will affect the annual depreciation charge and therefore the profit figure and balance sheet total.

(ii)   *Development costs* which satisfy certain criteria may be carried forward under SSAP 13 *Accounting for research and development* or written off in the year incurred. The accounting policy may vary between companies and, where significant amounts are involved, inter-company comparison would be meaningless without policy disclosure.

(iii)   *Stock* must be valued at the lower of cost and net realisable value in accordance with SSAP 9 *Stocks and long-term contracts*. The determination of cost will depend upon company policy, for example 'first in first out' (FIFO) or average cost. (Note that SSAP 9 does not allow 'last in first out' (LIFO). Stock is generally a significant figure in the financial statements so it is important for users to understand how it has been determined.

28 FRANCO

					£	£
(a)	(i)	DEBIT	Taxation charge		110,000	
		CREDIT	Taxation payable			110,000
			Being taxation charge for the year			

				£	£
	(ii)	DEBIT	Motor expenses	10,000	
		DEBIT	Wages	2,000	
		CREDIT	General expenses		12,000

	(iii)	DEBIT	Final dividend (appropriation account) (72 – 4 – 30)	38,000	
		DEBIT	Preference dividend (appropriation account)	4,000	
		CREDIT	Dividends proposed		42,000

	(iv)	DEBIT	Loan interest (P&L)	2,000	
		CREDIT	Interest payable		2,000

	(v)	DEBIT	Audit fees (P&L)	9,000	
		CREDIT	Accruals		9,000

	(vi)	No adjustment is needed
	(vii)	No adjustment is needed
	(viii)	No adjustment is needed
	(ix)	No adjustment is needed
	(x)	No adjustment is needed

(b) FRANCO LIMITED
PROFIT AND LOSS ACCOUNT FOR THE YEAR ENDED 31 MARCH 20X5

	Note	£'000
Turnover		
Continuing operations		2,460
Cost of sales		999
Gross profit		1,461
Distribution costs		416
Administrative expenses		341
Operating profit		
Continuing operations		704
Interest payable and similar charges		2
Profit on ordinary activities before taxation		702
Tax on profit on ordinary activities		110
Profit on ordinary activities after taxation		592
Dividends		72
Retained profit for the financial year		520

FRANCO LIMITED
BALANCE SHEET AS AT MARCH 20X5

	Note	£'000	£'000
Fixed assets			608
Current assets			
Stocks		225	
Debtors		447	
Cash at bank and in hand		7	
		679	
Creditors: amounts falling due within one year		337	
			342
Total assets less current liabilities			950
Creditors: amounts falling due after more than one year			
Long term loan			20
			930
Capital and reserves			
Called up share capital			250
Profit and loss account			680
			930

Workings

1   *Turnover*

	£'000
Per ETB	2,470
Less returns inwards	10
	2,460

2   Cost of sales

Opening stocks	215
Purchases	1,000
Plus carriage inwards	14
Less returns outwards	(5)
	1,224
Less closing stocks	225
	999

3   *Distribution costs and administrative expenses*

		Administrative expenses £	Distribution costs £
Depreciation:	buildings	3,000	1,000
	fixtures and fittings	4,000	1,000
	motor vehicles	2,000	8,000
	Office	1,000	-
Insurance (75/25)		9,000	3,000
Rates		10,000	10,000
Light and heat		18,000	18,000
Audit		9,000	-
Advertising		-	95,000
Increase in provision for doubtful debts		3,000	
General expenses (135 – 12)		100,000	23,000
Motor expenses (27 + 10)		10,000	27,000
Directors' emoluments		68,000	30,000
Salaries and wages (400 – 98 + 2)		104,000	200,000
		341,000	416,000

4   *Debtors*

	£'000
Trade debtors	450
Less provision for doubtful debts	(9)
	441
Prepayments	6
	447

5   *Fixed assets*

	Cost £'000	Accum depn £'000	Net book value £'000
Land and buildings	575	24	551
Fixtures and fittings	35	23	12
Motor vehicles	94	64	30
Office equipment	20	5	15
	724	116	608

6   *Creditors: amounts falling due within one year*

	£'000
Trade creditors	170
Corporation tax payable	110
Dividends proposed	42
Accruals (4 + 9)	13
Interest payable	2
	337

7   *Share capital*

	£'000
400,000 ordinary shares of 50p	200
50,000 preference shares of £1	50
	250

8   Profit and loss account

	£'000
As at 1 April 20X4	160
Retained profit for the year	520
As at 31 March 20X5	680

(c)

REPORT

To:	The Directors
	Franco Ltd
From:	Accounting Technician

Date: 5 April 20X5

Stock valuation and filing exemptions

(i)   *Stock valuation*

SSAP 9 states that stocks must be valued at the lower of cost and net realisable value.

Cost is that expenditure which has been incurred in the normal course of business in bringing the product or service to its present location and condition. This expenditure should include:

(1)   cost of purchase (including import duties, transport and handling costs and any other directly attributable costs, less trade discounts, rebates and subsidies);

(2) any costs of conversion appropriate to that location and condition, including direct labour and expenses and attributable production overheads.

Net realisable value is the actual or estimated selling price (net of trade but before settlement discounts) less:

(1) All further costs to completion
(2) All costs to be incurred in marketing, selling and distributing

Comparison of cost and net realisable value should be made for each item or category of stock separately rather than comparing total cost with total NRV.

(ii) *Filing exemptions*

Small and medium-sized companies are allowed certain 'filing exemptions': the accounts they lodge with the registrar of companies, and which are available for public inspection need not contain all the information which must be published by large companies.

A company qualifies as a *small* company in a particular financial year, if, for that year, at least two out of the following three limits are not exceeded.

Turnover	Balance sheet total	Average number of employees
£2.8 million	£1.4 million	50

For a medium sized company, the conditions (at least two of which must be satisfied) are as follows.

Turnover	Balance sheet total	Average number of employees
≤ £11.2 million	≤ £5.6 million	≤ 250

Small companies may file an abbreviated balance sheet showing only the items which, in the statutory format, are denoted by a letter or roman number. No profit and loss account, directors' report or details of directors' emoluments need be filed, and only certain of the notes to the accounts need to be produced.

Medium-sized companies are not required to analyse turnover between class of business or geographical market and the profit and loss account may begin with the figure of gross profit.

Public companies, banking and insurance companies, companies authorised under the Financial Services Act 1986 or members of a group containing any of these may not file abbreviated accounts.

Franco Ltd, by the above definitions, qualifies as a small company.

(d)

MEMORANDUM

To: The Directors
Franco Ltd
From: Accounting Technician   Date: 3 April 20X5

Accounting treatment

(i) *Issue of shares at a premium*

When shares are issued at an amount which exceeds their nominal value, the excess must be credited to a share premium account (s 130 CA 85) to which certain restrictions apply. Accordingly the required bookkeeping entries for the shares issued on 10 April will be as follows.

		£	£
DEBIT	Bank	37,500	
CREDIT	Ordinary share capital (50p × 50,000)		25,000
	Share premium (25p × 50,000)		12,500

(ii) This situation, where a debtor goes into liquidation after the balance sheet date, is one which is specifically mentioned in the appendix to SSAP 17 *Accounting for post balance sheet events* as an 'adjusting post balance sheet event'. Adjusting post balance sheet events are defined in the SSAP as 'post balance sheet events which provide additional evidence of conditions existing at the balance sheet date', and consequently require the relevant amounts in the financial statements to be changed. In this case the debt of £30,000 would need to be written off. The bookkeeping entries would be:

DEBIT	Bad debts	£30,000	
CREDIT	Debtors		£30,000

(iii) The situation described here is covered by FRS 12 *Provisions, contingent liabilities and contingent assests*. A contingent asset is defined a 'a possible asset that arises from past events and whose existence will only be confirmed by the occurrence of one or more uncertain future events not wholly within the entitys control'.

It follows from the above definition that the probable inflow of £25,000 from the legal suit is a 'contingent asset'. FRS 12 states that if a contingent asset is probable, it should be disclosed by way of a note in the financial statements. It cannot be recognised or it would not be a *contingent* asset.

(e) (i) 'Window dressing' techniques to improve the cash balance might include the following.

(1) Personal money is paid into the company bank account just before the year end to boost the cash balance, then withdrawn just after the year end.

(2) A large cheque is written against one group company's positive bank balance in favour of another group company with a large overdraft. The cheque is put through at the year end and then cancelled at the beginning of the next year, thus concealing the overdraft in the consolidated balance sheet (where positive and negative bank balances cannot be netted off).

(ii) 'Window dressing' is not defined in SSAP 17 *Accounting for post balance sheet events*. However, the SSAP does address the problem by requiring disclosure of the reversal or maturity after the year end of transactions entered into before the year end, the substance of which was primarily to alter the appearance of the company's balance sheet.

29   LAWNDERER

(a)   (i)   (1)

			£'000	£'000
	DEBIT	Sales	187	
	CREDIT	Disposals		187
	DEBIT	Disposals	491	
	CREDIT	Motor vehicles (cost)		491
	DEBIT	Motor vehicles (acc depn)	368	
	CREDIT	Disposals		368
	DEBIT	Disposals	64	
	CREDIT	P & L profit on disposal		64
(2)	DEBIT	Salesmen's commission	52	
	CREDIT	Accruals		52
(3)	DEBIT	Interest on debentures	153	
	CREDIT	Accruals		153
(4)	DEBIT	Tax charge	843	
	CREDIT	Corporation tax payable		843
(5)	DEBIT	Dividends	200	
	CREDIT	Dividends payable		200
(6)	DEBIT	Goodwill amortisation	36	
	CREDIT	Goodwill		36
(7)	DEBIT	Bad debt expense (115 – 78)	37	
	CREDIT	Provision for doubtful debts		37

(ii)   CALCULATION OF NEW RETAINED PROFIT

		£'000	£'000
Profit per extended trial balance			2,456
Add:	profit on disposal of motor vehicle		64
			2,520
Less:	deduction from sales	187	
	salesmen's commission	52	
	interest	153	
	tax	843	
	dividends	200	
	goodwill	36	
	bad debt expense	37	
			1,508
New retained profit			1,012

(b) LAWNDERER LIMITED
BALANCE SHEET AS AT 30 SEPTEMBER 20X5

	£'000	£'000
Fixed assets		
Intangible assets (360 – 36)		324
Tangible assets (W1)		2,827
		3,151
Current assets		
Stocks	4,572	
Debtors (W2)	2,531	
Cash at bank and in hand	3	
	7,106	
Creditors: amounts falling due within one year (W3)	4,679	
Net current assets		2,427
Total assets less current liabilities		5,578
Creditors: amounts falling due after more than one year		
9% debentures		3,400
		2,178

	£'000	£'000
Capital and reserves		
Called up share capital		1,000
Share premium		300
Profit and loss account (1,012 – 134)		878
		2,178

Workings

1 *Tangible fixed assets*

	Land and Buildings £'000	Fixtures and fittings £'000	Motor vehicles £'000	Office Equipment £'000	Total £'000
Cost 1/10/X4	1,875	576	1,200	244	3,895
	–	–	(491)	–	
	1,875	576	1,200	244	3,895
Accumulated depreciation 1/10/X4	83	214	644	83	
Charge for year	18	72	298	24	
Disposal			(368)		
	101	286	574	107	1,068
Net book value 30/9/X5					2,827

2 *Debtors*

	£'000
Trade debtors per ETB	2,603
Less provision for doubtful debts	115
	2,488
	43
Add: prepayments	2,531

3 *Creditors: amounts falling due within one year*

	£'000
Trade creditors	2,967
Bank overdraft	362
Corporation tax	843
Dividends	200
Accruals (101 + 52 + 153)	307
	4,679

(c) (i) The cost of developing the new lawnmower may be classified as development expenditure, defined by SSAP 13 *Accounting for research and development* as expenditure 'directed towards the introduction or improvement of specific products or processes.

Only development expenditure may be capitalised and then only if it satisfies all of the following conditions.

(1) There is a clearly defined project.

(2) The relevant expenditure is clearly and separately identifiable.

(3) The project is considered to be technically, environmentally and commercially feasible.

(4) The expenditure (including any future expenditure) is expected to be more than recoverable from the future revenues that will flow from the project.

(5) Adequate physical and human resources exist to complete the project.

(6) Management has made a decision to allocate the necessary resources to the project.

Of the above criteria, it would appear that only (v) - resources is in doubt. The directors will need to ascertain whether the necessary finance can be obtained, either from the bank or from the shareholders.

If the money is forthcoming, the development costs may, under SSAP 13, be capitalised and carried forward in the balance sheet until the project commences commercial production. The costs will then be amortised against future profits. The effect of this is that costs will not affect profits until production commences and sales are made.

(ii) The gearing of a company is a measure of the proportion of a company's capital that is long-term debt, carrying a right to a fixed return. It may be calculated as:

$$\frac{\text{Long–term debt}}{\text{Total capital}}$$

In Lawnderer Ltd, the gearing ratio works out as $\dfrac{3,400}{5,578} = 61\%$.

A company with a gearing ratio of more than 50% may be said to be high geared, although there is no absolute limit to what a gearing ratio ought to be. The problem with a high geared company is that, by definition, there is a lot of debt. Debt generally carries a fixed rate of interest, hence there is a given amount to be paid out from holders of debt before arriving at a residue available for distribution to the holders of equity. This makes the investment more risky for the equity shareholders.

(d) A directors' report will contain, among others, the following items. (*Note.* You are asked for only *four* of them.)

(i) A fair review of the development of the business of the company and its subsidiary undertakings during the year and of the subsidiaries' position at the end of it.

(ii) The principal activities of the company and its subsidiaries in the course of the financial year, and any significant changes in those activities during the year.

(iii) Where significant, an estimate should be provided of the difference between the book value of land held as fixed assets and its realistic market value.

(iv) Information about the company's policy for the employment of disabled persons:

        (1)   the policy for giving fair consideration to applications for jobs from disabled persons;

        (2)   the policy for continuing to employ (and train) people who have become disabled whilst employed by the company;

        (3)   the policy for the training, career development and promotion of disabled employees.

(Companies with fewer than 250 employees are exempt from (d).)

(v)   The names of persons who were directors at any time during the financial year.

(vi)   For those persons who are directors at the year end, the interests of each (or of their spouse or infant children) in shares or debentures of the company or subsidiaries:

        (1)   at the beginning of the year, or at the date of appointment as director, if this occurred during the year; and

        (2)   at the end of the year.

        If a director has no such interests at either date, this fact must be disclosed. (The information in (f) may be shown as a note to the accounts instead of in the directors' report.)

(vii)   A recent amendment to the Companies Act 1985 requires larger public companies to disclose details of the company's policy on the payment of creditors.

30   DOWANGO

(a)

				£'000	£'000
(i)	DEBIT	Dividends (500,000 × 6p)		30	
	CREDIT	Dividends payable			30
(ii)	DEBIT	Tax charge (P & L)		211	
	CREDIT	Corporation tax payable			211
(iii)	DEBIT	Interest payable (P & L)		15	
	CREDIT	Accruals (300 × 10% × 6/12)			15
(iv)	DEBIT	Distribution costs		19	
	CREDIT	Accruals			19
(v)	DEBIT	Administrative expenses		8	
	CREDIT	Investments (64 – 56)			8

(b) DOWANGO LIMITED
PROFIT AND LOSS ACCOUNT FOR THE YEAR ENDED 31 MARCH 20X6

	£'000
Turnover (W1)	
Continuing operations	5352
Cost of sales (W2)	2,910
Gross profit	2,442
Distribution costs (1,104 + 19)	1,123
Administrative expenses (709 + 8)	717
Operating profit	
Continuing operations	602
Interest payable and similar charge (15 + 15)	30
Profit on ordinary activities before taxation	572
Tax on profit on ordinary activities	211
Profit on ordinary activities after tax	361
Dividends (20 + 30)	50
Retained profit for the year	311

DOWNGO LIMITED
BALANCE SHEET AS AT 31 MARCH 20X6

	£'000	£'000
Fixed assets		
Tangible assets (W3)		1,153
Current assets		
Investment	56	
Stock	365	
Debtors (W4)	613	
Cash at bank and in hand	3	
	1,037	
Creditors: amounts falling due within one year (W5)	804	
Net current assets		233
Total assets less current liabilities		1,386
Creditors: amounts falling due after more than one year		300
		1,086
Capital and reserves		
Called up share capital		500
Profit and loss account (275 + 311)		586
		1,086

Workings

1   *Turnover*

	£'000
Sales	5,391
Less returns inwards	39
	5,352

2   *Cost of sales*

	£'000
Opening stock	298
Purchases	2,988
Carriage inwards	20
Less returns outwards	(31)
	3,275
Less closing stock	365
	2,910

3   *Fixed assets*

	Cost	Acc. depn.	NBV
	£'000	£'000	£'000
Land	431	-	431
Buildings	512	184	328
Fixtures and fittings	389	181	208
Motor vehicles	341	204	137
Office equipment	105	56	49
	1,778	625	1,153

4   *Debtors*

	£'000
Trade debtors	619
Less provision	27
	592
Prepayments	21
	613

5   *Creditors: amounts due within one year*

	£'000
Trade creditors	331
Bank overdraft	157
Accruals (41 + 15 + 19)	75
Dividends payable	30
Corporation tax payable	211
	804

(c)

MEMO

To:	The directors
	Dowango Ltd
From:	AAT Student
Date:	30 April 20X6
Subject:	Accounts of Dowango Ltd

(i)   (1)   It is certainly possible to show the land and buildings at valuation rather than cost. Although the Companies Act 1985 states that the normal basis for the preparation of financial statements should be historical cost principles, under the alternative accounting rules, assets may be revalued.

(2) Under the alternative accounting rules the land would be shown at its valuation of £641,000 and the buildings at their valuation of £558,000. The difference between the net book value of the assets and their new valuation would be credited to a revaluation reserve, which is an undistributable reserve. The amounts to be credited to the revaluation reserve can be calculated as follows.

	Land £'000	Buildings £'000
Valuation	641	558
NBV	431	328
	210	230

(3) Gearing is a measure of how much long-term finance is in the form of long-term debt. If may be calculated as:

$$\frac{\text{Loan capital}}{\text{Total capital}}$$

Under the historical cost convention, total capital is £1,386,000. The gearing ratio may thus be calculated as:

$$\frac{300}{1,386} = 22\%$$

If the assets were revalued, the denominator of this ratio, ie total capital would increase by the amount credited to the revaluation reserve (£210,000 + 230,000 + £440,000). The gearing ratio would thus reduce to:

$$\frac{300}{1,826} = 16\%$$

It is possible that the lower gearing ratio may influence the bank's decision to lend the company the money to finance the acquisition. A lower gearing ratio means that the company is less risky from the bank's point of view. However, this may not be as significant when, as here, the company already has a low gearing ratio.

(4) In future years there will be an effect on the profit and loss account. Depreciation would be calculated on the revalued amount, which is greater than historical cost. Thus the depreciation charge will be higher.

(ii) Because the investment is a current asset - it was purchased with a view to resale - it must be valued at the lower of purchase price and net realisable value. This is in accordance with the prudence concept, which states that profits should not be anticipated but that foreseeable losses should be provided for. As we can foresee a loss on the sale of the investment, it should be shown at its realisable value of £56,000.

(iii) The rule for valuation of stock follows the prudence concept. It is set out is SSAP 9 *Stocks and long-term contracts*, which states that stock should be valued at the lower of cost and net realisable value. Furthermore, the comparison of cost and net realisable value should be done on an item by item basis, not on the total of all stocks, although similar items may be grouped together. Applying this policy would lead us to value the undervalued items at a cost of £340,000 and the overvalued items at the sales price of £15,000. The effect of this is to reduce the overall value of stock from £365,000 to £355,000 with the consequent effect of a £10,000 reduction in profit and assets.

(d) The ratios may be calculated as follows.

	Company A	Company B
Return on capital employed	$\dfrac{200}{600+400}=20\%$	$\dfrac{420}{1,700+1,100}=15\%$
Net profit margin	$\dfrac{200}{800}=25\%$	$\dfrac{420}{2,100}=20\%$
Asset turnover	$\dfrac{800}{1,000}=0.8$	$\dfrac{2,100}{2,800}=0.75$

Other ratios which might be useful include the following. (Note that you were asked for only *one* of these ratios.)

	Company A	Company B
Gross profit margin	$\dfrac{360}{800}=45\%$	$\dfrac{1,050}{2,100}=5\%$
Expenses: sales	$\dfrac{160}{800}=20\%$	$\dfrac{630}{2,100}=30\%$

Most of the profitability ratios indicate that Company A would be the better one to target. Return on capital employed, net profit margin and asset turnover are all higher for Company A. However, if gross profit margin is calculated, the reverse is true, and Company B appears more profitable. This suggests that it is overheads rather than underlying profitability where Company B falls short, as is confirmed when one calculates the expenses to sales ratio. The question of which company to target is therefore not clear cut. If Company B were taken over and if a more efficient management were able to keep costs down, it might prove to be the more profitable in the long run.

(e) If Dowango Ltd purchase the whole of a company's share capital, the latter company will become its subsidiary (assuming that Dowango Ltd has more than 50% of the voting rights.) Under FRS 2 *Accounting for subsidiary undertakings*, consolidated accounts would be required in addition to the accounts for the individual companies.

31 SPIRAES

(a)

			£'000	£'000
(i)	DEBIT	Dividends p&l	80	
	CREDIT	Dividends payable (b/s)		80
		$\pounds(1,000,000 \times 4 \times 0.02)$		
(ii)	DEBIT	Tax charge (p&l)	1,356	
	CREDIT	Corporation tax payable (b/s)		1,356
(iii)	DEBIT	Interest payable (p&l)	189	
	CREDIT	Interest payable (b/s)		189
		$\pounds4,200,000 \times 9\% \times 6/12$		
(iv)	DEBIT	Land	720	
	CREDIT	Revaluation reserve		720
		$\pounds(4,290,000 - 3,570,000)$		
(v)	DEBIT	Stock (p&l)	50	
	CREDIT	Stock (b/s)		50

(b) *Item (f) - revaluation of land*

Although the Companies Act 1985 states that the normal basis for the preparation of financial statements should be historical cost principles, under the alternative accounting rules, assets may be revalued.

Where the value of any fixed asset is determined by using the alternative accounting rules, the amount of profit or loss arising must be credited to a separate reserve, the revaluation reserve. The calculation of the relevant amounts should be based on the written down values of the assets prior to revelation. The year of valuation and the name of the valuer must be disclosed. Spiraes Ltd has adopted the alternative accounting rules and intends to show the land at valuation rather than at historical cost.

Item (h)- stock

The stock figure has been written down to reflect the fall in value. The main principle being applied here derives from SSAP 9 *Accounting for stocks and long-term contracts*. The SSAP states that stocks must be shown at the lower of cost and net realisable value. The stocks were sold for £355,000 after the year end, which provides evidence of their net realisable value at the year end.

The other relevant accounting standard is SSAP 17 *Accounting for post balance sheet events*. According to SSAP 17 this is an adjusting event, so the accounts must be adjusted to reflect the fall in value.

(c) SPIRAES LIMITED
PROFIT AND LOSS ACCOUNT
FOR THE YEAR ENDED 30 NOVEMBER 20X6

	£'000
Turnover (W1)	
Continuing operations	18,147
Cost of sales (W2)	10,230
Gross profit	7,917
Distribution costs	2,514
Administrative expenses	1,820
Operating profit	
Continuing operations	3,583
Income from other fixed asset investments	52
	3,635
Interest payable and similar charges (189 × 2)	378
Profit on ordinary activities before taxation	3,257
Tax on profit on ordinary activities	1,356
Profit for the financial year	1,901
Dividends (Task 1)	80
Retained profit for the financial year	1,821

Workings

1   *Turnover*

	£'000
Sales per ETB	18,742
Returns inwards	595
	18,147

2   *Cost of sales*

	£'000	£'000
Opening stock		3,871
Purchases	10,776	
Less returns outwards	314	
	10,462	
		14,333
Less closing stock		4,103
		10,230

(d) STATEMENT OF TOTAL RECOGNISED GAINS AND LOSSES

	£'000
Profit for the financial year	1,901
Unrealised surplus on revaluation of properties	720
	2,621

32   PRIMAVERA FASHIONS

> **Tutorial note.** This is the *company* balance sheet. Do not worry about any consolidation aspects!

(a) PRIMAVERA FASHIONS LIMITED
CORRECTED BALANCE SHEET AS AT 31 MARCH 20X7

	£'000	£'000
Fixed assets		
Intangible assets		128
Tangible assets (W1)		3,273
Investments		2,924
		6,325
Current assets		
Stocks	1,178	
Debtors (W2)	833	
Cash at bank and in hand	152	
	2,163	
Creditors: amounts falling due within one year (W3)	1,209	
Net current assets		954
Total assets less current liabilities		7,279
Creditors: amounts falling due after more than one year		(1,500)
		5,779
Capital and reserves		
Called up share capital		1,000
Share premium		800
Revaluation reserve		550
Profit and loss account (W4)		3,429
		5,779

Workings

1   *Fixed assets*

	Cost	Acc Depn	NBV
	£'000	£'000	£'000
Land	525	-	525
Buildings	1,000	220	780
Fixtures & fittings	1,170	346	824
Motor vehicles	1,520	583	937
Office equipment	350	143	207
	4,565	1,292	3,273

Note. The previous accountant deducted the depreciation for the year, rather than the accumulated depreciation.

2   *Debtors*

	£'000
Trade debtors	857
Less provision for doubtful debts	(61)
Plus pre-payments	37
	833

3   *Creditors: amounts falling due within one year*

	£'000
Trade creditors	483
Accounts	104
Corporation tax payable	382
Dividends payable	240
	1,209

4   *Profit and loss account*

	£'000
Profit for the year per ETB	1,232
Less final dividend	240
Less corporation tax charge	382
	610
Add Profit and Loss a/c at 1/6/96	2,819
Profit and Loss a/c at 31 March 20X7	3,429

(b) (i) (1) A share premium arises when a company sells shares for a price which is higher than the nominal value. By 'premium' is meant the difference between the issue price of the share and its nominal value. For example, the shares of Primavera Fashions Ltd could have been issued at a premium of 20p per share. The accounting entries would be:

		£'000	£'000
DEBIT	Cash	1,800	
CREDIT	Share capital (4,000,000 × 25p)		1,000
CREDIT	Share premium (4,000,000 × 20p)		800

(2) The share premium account is a statutory reserve. It is not available for the distribution of dividends.

(3) Possible uses of the share premium account include (any one of) the following.

- Issuing bonus shares
- Writing off preliminary expenses
- Expenses of issuing shares or debentures

(ii) The fact that the debtor went into liquidation after the end of the financial year will have an impact on the financial statements. Under SSAP 17 *Accounting for post balance sheet events*, this would be classified as an adjusting post-balance sheet event. Adjusting post balance sheet events are defined by SSAP 17 as 'post balance sheet events which provide additional evidence of conditions existing at the balance sheet date'.

The value of debtors in the balance sheet will be reduced by £24,000 and there will be a charge of £24,000 for bad debts in the profit and loss account.

(iii) (1) Spring Ltd is an associated company. The amount shown on the group balance sheet is therefore:

	£'000
Group share of net assets as at 31.3.X7	350
Premium paid on acquisition (W)	120
	470

Working: premium on acquisition

	£'000
Cost of investment	400
Group share of net assets (35% × 800,000)	280
Premium	120

Alternatively, the amount may be calculated as follows:

	£'000
Cost	400
Share of post-acquisition retained profits (35% £200,000)	70
	470

Only the *total* (£470,000) needs to appear in the consolidated balance sheet under the heading 'Investment in associated company'.

(2) On the notes, the investment in Spring Ltd will be analysed as follows.

	£'000
Share of net assets	350
Premium paid on acquisition	120
	470

33   DESKCOVER

(a) DESKCOVER LIMITED
PROFIT AND LOSS ACCOUNT
FOR THE YEAR ENDED 31 DECEMBER 20X7

	£'000
Turnover	
Continuing operations (W1)	20,317
Cost of sales (W2)	11,174
Gross profit	9,143
Distribution costs	3,756
Administrative expenses	2,981
Operating profit	
Continuing operations	2,406
Interest payable and similar charges (W3)	272
Profit on ordinary activities before taxation	2,134
Tax on profit on ordinary activities	726
Profit on ordinary activities after taxation	1,408
Dividends (W4)	560
Retained profit for the financial year	848

DESKCOVER LIMITED
BALANCE SHEET AS AT 31 DECEMBER 20X7

	£'000	£'000
Fixed assets		
Tangible assets (W5)		4,929
Investments		4,010
		8,939
Current assets		
Stocks	5,244	
Debtors (W6)	3,273	
Cash at bank and in hand	316	
	8,833	
Creditors: amounts falling due within one year (W7)	(3,335)	
Net current assets		5,498
Total assets less current liabilities		14,437
Creditors: amounts falling due after one year		
8% debentures		3,400
		11,037
Capital and reserves		
Called up share capital		4,000
Share premium		1,800
Profit and loss account (W8)		5,237
		11,037

Workings

1 *Turnover*

	£'000
Sales per ETB	20,469
Less returns inwards	152
	20,317

2 *Cost of sales*

	£'000	£'000
Opening stock	4,502	
Purchases	12,025	
Less returns outwards	(109)	
		16,418
Closing stock		5,244
Cost of sales		11,174

3 *Interest payable and similar charges*

Interest for year $= 136 \times \dfrac{12}{6} = £272,000$

4 Dividends

	£'000
Interim dividend	240
Final dividend proposed	320
$4,000,000 \times 0.08$	560

5 *Fixed assets*

	Cost	Acc depn	NBV
	£'000	£'000	£'000
Land	1,602	-	1,602
Buildings	2,137	627	1,510
Fixtures and fittings	1,399	754	645
Motor vehicles	1,786	903	883
Office equipment	402	113	289
	7,326	2,397	4,929

6 *Debtors*

	£'000
Trade debtors	3,386
Less provision for doubtful debts	169
	3,217
Prepayments	56
	3,273

7 *Creditors: amounts falling due within one year*

	£'000	£'000
Trade creditors		2,035
Proposed dividend (W4)		320
Corporation tax		726
Accruals: per ETB	118	
interest (W3)	136	
		254
		3,335

8 *Profit and loss account*

	£'000
At 1 January 20X7	4,389
Retained profit for the year	848
At 31 December 20X7	5,237

(b) (i) The treatment of this item is governed by SSAP 17 *Accounting for post balance sheet events*. The SSAP distinguishes between 'adjusting events' and 'non-adjusting events'. 'Adjusting events' are defined as events which 'provide additional evidence of conditions existing at the balance sheet date'.

The liquidation of the debtor clearly falls into the category of adjusting events, since it provides evidence about the debtors figure in the balance sheet, ie that it is less than anticipated. The financial statements of Underdesk Ltd for the year ended 31 December will need to be adjusted accordingly.

The accounts to be adjusted are debtors and provision for doubtful debts. The specific provision of £93,000 is no longer needed as the entire debt is to be written off. The double entry is as follows.

		£'000	£'000
DEBIT	Bad debt expenses	186	
CREDIT	Debtors		186
DEBIT	Provision for doubtful debts	93	

(ii) UNDERDESK LIMITED
RECONCILIATION OF OPERATING PROFIT
TO NET CASH INFLOW FROM OPERATING ACTIVITIES

	£'000
Operating profit	673
Depreciation	672
Profit on sale of tangible fixed assets	(29)
Increase in stock (607 – 543)	(64)
Increase in debtors (481 – 426)	(55)
Increase in creditors (371 – 340)	31
Net cash inflow from operating activities	1,228

(iii) UNDERDESK LIMITED
CASH FLOW STATEMENT FOR THE YEAR ENDED 31 DECEMBER 20X7

	£'000
Net cash inflow from operating activities	1,228
Returns on investment and servicing of finance	
Interest paid	(156)
Taxation (W1)	(124)
Capital expenditure	
Payments to acquire tangible fixed assets (W2)	(3,239)
Receipts from sale of fixed assets	114
	(2,177)
Equity dividends paid	(96)
Financing	(2,273)
Loan (1,700 – 520)	1,180
Issue of share capital (1,400 – 800)	600
Share premium (400 – 100)	300
Decrease in cash	(193)

Workings

1   *Taxation*

	£'000		£'000
		Bal b/d 1.1.X7	124
Cash paid	124	Profit and loss account	129
Bal c/d 31.12.X7	129		
	253		253

2   *Payments to acquire tangible fixed assets*

FIXED ASSETS

	£'000		£'000
Bal b/d 1.1.X7	2,979	Disposals (187 – 102)	85
Additions (bal fig)	3,239	Depreciation	672
		Bal c/d 31.12.X7	5,461
	6,218		6,218

(iv) Calculation of goodwill arising on acquisition of Underdesk Ltd

	£'000	£'000
Consideration		4,010
Share of net assets acquired		
Share capital	1,400	
Share premium	400	
Revaluation reserve (5,761 – 5,461)	300	
Profit and loss account	2,280	
	4,380	
Group share: 75%		3,285
		725

The treatment of goodwill arising on consolidation is governed by FRS 10 *Goodwill and intangible assets*. Under FRS 10, positive purchased goodwill should initially be capitalised and classed as an asset at cost. It should then be amortised on a systematic basis over its useful economic life. If it is considered that the economic life is indefinite, no amortisation is needed.

FRS 10 presumes that goodwill has a life of 20 years or less, but accepts that this presumption is rebuttable. This, however, puts the onus on the reporting entity to demonstrate that not only does the asset have an extended life but that its value is capable of an annual impairment review.

34 SOLU

> **Tutorial note**. Make sure you know how to deal with revaluations on consolidation. This is particularly important for the minority interest in Part (d).

(a) The journal entries required are as follows.

	Debit £'000	Credit £'000
Dividends (p&l) (£400,000 × 4 × (0.06 – 0.02)	64	
Dividends payable		64
Corporation tax (p&l)	75	
Corporation tax (creditor)		75
Interest charge (p&l) (10% × £200,000 × 6/12)	10	
Accruals		10
Bad debt expense (W)	9	
Provision for bad debts		9

Working: Bad debt expense

Debtors per ETB	£500,000
Provision required = £500,000 × 2% =	£10,000
∴ Increase in provision = (10 – 1) =	£9,000

(b) SOLU LIMITED
PROFIT AND LOSS ACCOUNT FOR THE YEAR ENDED 31 MARCH 20X8

	£'000
Turnover (continuing operations)	4,090
Cost of sales (W1)	1,805
Gross profit	2,285
Distribution costs	1,055
Administrative expenses (W2)	999
Operating profit (continuing operations)	231
Interest payable and similar charges (W3)	20
Profit on ordinary activities before taxation	211
Tax on profit on ordinary activities	75
Profit on ordinary activities after taxation	136
Dividends (32+64)	96
Retained profit for the financial year	40

Workings

1 *Cost of sales*

	£'000
Opening stock	300
Purchases	1,800
Carriage inwards	25
Closing stock	(320)
	1,805

2 *Administrative expenses*

	£'000
Per ETB	990
Increase in bad debt prov'n	9
	999

3   *Interest payable*

	£'000
Per ETB	10
Accrual	10
	20

(c)

NOTES TO THE DIRECTORS

(i)   *Land at valuation*

The Companies Act 1985 permits fixed assets to be shown at valuation rather than cost, as does the new accounting standard, FRS 15 *Tangible fixed assets*. The increase is calculated as follows.

	£'000
NBV per ETB (268 – 50)	218
Valuation	550
Increase in value	332

The entries required to adjust the accounts are as follows.

DEBIT	Land and buildings	£332,000	
CREDIT	Revaluation reserve		£332,000

Depreciation must be charged on the revalued amount.

(ii)   *Accruals concept*

Under SSAP 2 *Disclosure of accounting policies*, revenue and costs are *accrued*. This means that they are recognised as they are earned or incurred, not as money is received or paid. They are matched with one another and dealt with in the profit and loss account of the period to which they relate.

A clear example from the accounts of Solu which illustrates the accruals concept is the accrual for six months' interest on the long-term loan. While no money has been paid out, this charge has been incurred in the last six months of 20X8 and must therefore be matched against the profits of that year.

(iii)   *Subsidiary undertaking*

A company (S) is a subsidiary of its parent (H) in the following circumstances.

(1)   H holds a majority of the voting rights in S.

(2)   H is a member of S and had the right to appoint or remove directors holding a majority of the voting rights at meetings of the board.

(3)   H has a right to exercise a dominant influence over S by virtue of the memorandum or articles or a control contract.

(4)   H is a member of S and controls alone, or under an agreement with other shareholders or members, a majority of the voting rights in S.

(5)   H has a participating interest in S and actually exercises a dominant influence over S or is managed on a unified basis with S.

(6)   S is a subsidiary of a subsidiary of H.

(d)   *Minority interest in the Solu Group as at 31 March 20X8*

	£'000	
Share capital	100	
Share premium	50	
Profit and loss account	25	
Revaluation reserve (W)	25	
	200	× 25% = £50,000

Working: revaluation reserve

	£'000
Valuation at 31.3.X8	95
NBV	70
Revaluation reserve	25

35   BATHLEA

> **Tutorial note**. In Part (c) your answer should be in terms of FRS 12 *Provisions, contingent liabilities and contingent assets*.

(a)   The journal entries required are as follows.

	Debit £'000	Credit £'000
Dividends (p&l) (£500,000 × 5.5)	27.5	
Dividends payable		27.5
Corporation tax (p&l)	11	
Corporation tax (creditor)		11
Interest charge (p&l) (12% × £100,000 × 1/12)	1	
Accruals		1
Bad debt expense	10	
Debtors		10
Bad debt expense (W)	5.8	
Provision for bad debts		5.8

Working: Increase in bad debt provision

	£'000
Debtors per ETB	370
Less bad debt written off	(10)
Adjusted debtors at 30.9.X8	360
Provision required (3% × 360)	10.8
Existing provision	(5.0)
∴ Increase in provision	5.8

(b)   BATHLEA LIMITED
PROFIT AND LOSS ACCOUNT FOR THE YEAR ENDED 31 SEPTEMBER 20X8

	£'000
Turnover (continuing operations)	3,509.0
Cost of sales (W1)	1,641.0
Gross profit	1868.0
Distribution costs	857.0
Administrative expenses (W2)	907.8
Operating profit (continuing operations)	103.2
Interest payable and similar charges (11+1)	12.0
Profit on ordinary activities before taxation	91.2
Tax on profit on ordinary activities	11.0
Profit on ordinary activities after taxation	80.2
Dividends (15+27.5)	42.5
Retained profit for the financial year	37.7

BATHLEA LIMITED
BALANCE SHEET AS AT 31 SEPTEMBER 20X8

	£'000	£'000
Fixed assets		
Tangible assets (W3)		500.0
Current assets		
Stocks	250.0	
Debtors (W4)	359.2	
	609.2	
Creditors: amounts falling due within one year (W5)	401.5	
		207.7
Total assets less current liabilities		707.7
Creditors: amounts falling due after more than one year		100.0
		607.7
Capital and reserves		
Called up share capital		500.0
Profit and loss account (W6)		107.7
		607.7

Workings

1 *Cost of sales*

	£'000
Opening stock	200
Purchases	1,600
Carriage inwards	91
Closing stock	(250)
	1,641

2 *Administrative expenses*

	£'000
Per ETB	892.0
Bad debt written off	10.0
Increase in bad debt provision	5.8
	907.8

3 *Fixed assets*

	Cost	Acc. depn.	NBV
	£'000	£'000	£'000
Land and buildings	300	65	235
Fixtures and fittings	220	43	177
Motor vehicles	70	27	43
Office equipment	80	35	45
	670	170	500

4 *Debtors*

	£'000
Per ETB	370.0
Bad debt written off	(10.0)
Bad debt provision	(10.8)
Prepayment	10.0
	359.2

5   *Creditors: amounts falling due within one year*

	£'000
Per ETB	350.0
Accruals (9 + 1)	10.0
Taxation	11.0
Dividends	27.5
Bank overdraft	3.0
	401.5

6   Profit and loss account

	£'000
Profit and loss account b/f	70.0
Profit for the year	37.7
Profit and loss account c/f	107.7

(c)

NOTES FOR DIRECTORS ON ACCOUNTING STANDARDS

(i)   *Law suit*

The law suit is a contingent liability and, as such is governed by FRS 12 *Provisions, contingent liabilities and contingent assets*. FRS 12 defines a contingent liability as:

'A possible obligation that arises from past events and whose existence will be confirmed only by the occurrence or non-occurrence of one or more uncertain future events not wholly within the entity's control'.

Under FRS 12, a contingent liability should never be accrued for in the accounts – if the outflow is probable, the item is a provision. If the outflow is merely possible, a contingent liability should be disclosed. However, in this case the possibility of an outflow is remote so there is no need to disclose or provide.

(ii)   *Development expenditure*

The treatment of development expenditure is governed by SSAP 13 *Accounting for research and development*. The standard states that development expenditure is incurred with a particular commercial aim in view and in the reasonable expectation of earning profits or reducing costs. It is therefore appropriate that in these circumstances development costs should be deferred (capitalised) and matched against the future revenues.

Development costs may, however, only be capitalised when certain strict criteria are met.

(1)   There is a clearly defined project and the related expenditure is separately identifiable.

(2)   The project is technically feasible and commercially viable.

(3)   All further costs will be more than covered by related future revenues.

(4)   The company has adequate resources to complete the project.

Where development expenditure is capitalised, its amortisation should begin with the commercial production of the product, and should be written off over the period in which the product is expected to be sold.

36 CLAUDE

Tutorial note. This question does not ask you to produce a cash flow statement, but instead for the most important note to the statement. You should have plenty of time left, for part (b), the discussion question

(a) RECONCILIATION OF OPERATING PROFIT
    TO NET CASH INFLOW FROM OPERATING ACTIVITIES

	£'000
Operating profit	961
Depreciation	352
Profit on sale of tangible fixed assets	(75)
Increase in stock	(106)
Increase in debtors	(199)
Increase in creditors	49
Net cash inflow from operating activities	982

(b)   MEMORANDUM

To: The directors
        Claude Ltd
From: A N Assistant
Date: 6 January 20X3
Subject: Cash flow statement

It has been argued that 'profit' does not always give a useful or meaningful picture of a company's operations. Readers of a company's financial statements might even be misled by a reported profit figure.

(i)   Shareholders might believe that if a company makes a profit after tax, of say, £100,000 then this is the amount which it could afford to pay as a dividend. Unless the company has sufficient cash available to stay in business and also to pay a dividend, the shareholders' expectations would be wrong.

(ii)   Employees might believe that if a company makes profits, it can afford to pay higher wages next year. This opinion may not be correct: the ability to pay wages depends on the availability of cash.

(iii)   Survival of a business entity depends not so much on profits as on its ability to pay its debts when they fall due. Such payments might include 'profit and loss' items such as material purchases, wages, interest and taxation etc, but also capital payments for new fixed assets and the repayment of loan capital when this falls due (for example on the redemption of debentures).

From these examples, it may be apparent that a company's performance and prospects depend not so much on the 'profits' earned in a period, but more realistically on liquidity or *cash flows*.

The cash flow statement gives an indication of the relationship between profitability and cash-generating ability, and thus of the quality of the profit earned. It can assist in predicting the future cash flows of a business.

37   BARK

> **Tutorial note**. This question is straightforward, but remember that a high level of accuracy is required in a central assessment. The only tricky bit is the calculation of the purchase of fixed assets. Study our solution carefully

(a)   CASH FLOW STATEMENT OF BARK LIMITED
       FOR YEAR ENDED 31 MARCH 20X4.

	£'000
Net cash inflow from operating activities	716
Returns on investments and servicing of finance	
Interest paid	(66)
Taxation	(181)
Capital expenditure	
Payments to acquire tangible fixed assets	(753)
Sale of asset	101
	(183)
Equity dividends paid	(65)
	(248)
Financing	
Repayment of loan	(18)
Issue of ordinary share capital	100
Decrease in cash	(166)

(b)   *Reconciliation between the cash flows from operating activities and the operating profit*

	£'000
Operating profit	739
Depreciation charges	253
Profit on sale of tangible fixed assets	(35)
Increase in stock	(111)
Increase in debtors	(2)
Decrease in creditors	(128)
Net cash inflow from operating activities	716

Workings

1   *Taxation*

TAXATION

	£'000		£'000
Cash	181	Opening balance	132
Closing balance	186	Profit and loss	235
	367		367

2   *Purchases of fixed assets*

	£'000
Difference between opening and closing balances on fixed assets	434
Net book value of assets sold	66
Depreciation	253
Assets purchased	753

ie £1,340 + 753 – 253 –66 = £1,774

The cash outflow from purchase of fixed assets is thus £753,000

3   *Dividends*

DIVIDENDS

	£'000		£'000
Cash	65	Opening balance	65
Closing balance	85	Profit and loss	85
	140		140

38 FUN AND GAMES

(a) GAMES LIMITED
RECONCILIATION OF OPERATING PROFIT
TO NET CASH INFLOW FROM OPERATING ACTIVITIES

	£'000
Operating profit (246 + 56)	302
Depreciation	277
Increase in stocks (918 – 873)	(45)
Increase in debtors (751 – 607)	(144)
Increase in creditors (583 – 512)	71
Net cash inflow from operating activities	461

(b) NOTES FOR BOARD MEETING ON MINORITY INTEREST

(i) *Calculation of minority interest*

	£'000
Share capital	1,000
Share premium	100
Profit and loss account	1,180
Revaluation reserve (W)	200
	2,480 × 25% = £620,000

Working: Revaluation reserve	£'000
Book value of fixed assets	1,845
Fair value of fixed assets	2,045
Difference to revaluation reserve	200

(ii) *Presentation of minority interest*

The minority interest will be disclosed as part of share capital and reserves, separately after the share capital and reserves attributable to the group.

(iii) *Definition of minority interest*

FRS 2 *Accounting for subsidiary undertakings* defines a minority interest as the interest in a subsidiary undertaking included in the consolidation that is attributable to the shares held by persons other than the parent undertaking and its subsidiaries.

39 GEORGE

Tutorial note. You should have realised that Part (b) has to be done first to arrive at the net cash inflows from operating activities in Part (a).

(a) GEORGE LIMITED

CASH FLOW STATEMENT FOR THE YEAR ENDED 31 MARCH 20X5

	£'000	£'000
Net cash inflow from operating activities		350
Returns on investment and servicing of finance		
Interest paid		((20)
Taxation		
Corporation tax paid (20X4)		(21)
Capital expenditure		
Purchase of fixed asset	(110)	
Receipts from sale of fixed assets (W)	7	
		(103)
		206
Equity dividends paid		(30)
		176
Financing		
Issue of ordinary share capital (40 – 25)	15	
Long term loan (200 – 100)	100	
Redemption of debentures	(500)	
Net cash outflow from financing		(385)
Decrease in cash		(209)

(b) *Reconciliation of operating profit to net cash flow from operating activities*

	£'000
Operating profit	237
Depreciation	275
Profit on sales of fixed assets	(2)
Increase in stocks (210 – 200)	(10)
Increase in debtors (390 – 250)	(140)
Decrease in creditors (150 – 160)	(10)
Net cash inflow from operating activities	350

Working: Receipts from sale of fixed assets

DISPOSALS OF FIXED ASSETS

	£		£
Fixed assets (cost)	10,000	Accumulated depreciation	5,000
Profit on sale	2,000	Proceeds (bal fig)	7,000
	12,000		12,000

40 CASHEDIN

CASHEDIN LIMITED
CASH FLOW STATEMENT FOR THE YEAR ENDED 30 SEPTEMBER 20X5

	£'000	£'000
Net cash inflow from operating activities		104
Returns on investments and servicing of finance		
Interest paid		(218)
Taxation		(75)
		(189)
Capital expenditure		
Payments to acquire tangible fixed assets	(358)	
Proceeds from sale of fixed assets	132	
		(226)
		(415)
Equity dividends paid		(280)
		(695)
Financing		
Loans	200	
Issue of ordinary share capital	150	
		350
Decrease in cash		(345)

Reconciliation of operating profit and net cash inflow from operating activities

	£'000
Operating profit	24
Depreciation	318
Increase in stock	(251)
Increase in debtors	(152)
Increase in creditors	165
Net cash inflow from operating activities	104

41 POISED

POISED LIMITED
RECONCILIATION OF OPERATING PROFIT
TO NET CASH INFLOW FROM OPERATING ACTIVITIES

	£'000
Operating profit	2,099
Depreciation	1,347
Increase in stocks (2,473 – 2,138)	(335)
Increase in debtors (1,872 – 1,653)	(219)
Increase in creditors (1,579 – 1,238)	341
Net cash inflow from operating activities	3,233

42 EDLIN

> **Tutorial note**. The trickiest part of the cash flow statement, assuming you're familiar with the method, is the fixed asset working. Study our solution carefully if you slipped up. In part (c) you are asked to *comment* on the ratios as well as calculating them – make sure you do this.

(a) EDLIN LIMITED
RECONCILIATION OF OPERATING PROFIT
TO NET CASH INFLOW FROM OPERATING ACTIVITIES

	£'000
Operating profit	650
Depreciation	175
Profit on sale of asset	(5)
Increase in stocks	(20)
Increase in debtors	(90)
Increase in creditors	40
Net cash inflow from operating activities	750

(b) EDLIN LIMITED
CASH FLOW STATEMENT FOR THE YEAR ENDED 31 MARCH 20X8

	£'000
Net cash inflow from operating activities	750
Returns oninvestment and servicing of finance	
Interest paid	((15)
Taxation (20X7 creditor, paid y/e 31.3.X8)	(35)
Capital expenditure and financial investment (Note 1)	(522)
	178
Equity dividends paid (20X7 creditor, paid y/e 31.3.X8)	(50)
	128
Financing (Note 1)	70
Increase in cash	198

Note 1: Gross cash flows

Capital expenditure and financial investment

	£'000
Proceeds of sale of fixed asset (W)	13
Purchase of fixed assets	(535)
	(522)

Financing

	£'000
Issue of shares	
Share capital	20
Share premium	20
	40
Increase in loan (150 – 120)	30
	70

Working: Proceeds of sale of fixed asset

	£'000
Net book value: $20 - (20 \times 3/5)$	8
Profit	5
∴ Proceeds	13

(c)

Gearing ratio

	20X8	20X7
$\dfrac{\text{Long - term loan}}{\text{Long - term loan plus capital and reserves}}$	$\dfrac{150}{150 + 740} = 17\%$	$\dfrac{120}{120 + 265} = 31\%$

OR:

	20X8	20X7
$\dfrac{\text{Long - term loan}}{\text{Capital and reserves}}$	$\dfrac{150}{740} = 20\%$	$\dfrac{120}{265} = 45\%$

Current ratio

$\dfrac{\text{Current assets}}{\text{Current liabilities}}$	$\dfrac{688}{350} = 2.0$	$\dfrac{380}{195} = 1.9$

Comments

The gearing ratio, whichever way it is calculated has decreased significantly in 20X8. This is because, although the loan has increased, this has been more than offset by an increase in share capital and reserves. Since a high-geared company can be a more risky investment, it is comforting to know that Edlin Ltd is financing its expansion from a variety of sources other than debt.

The current ratio is more or less unchanged. Again this is a good sign. The company is expanding, and this can sometimes lead to overtrading. Edlin Ltd clearly has this under control.

43 PRACTICE QUESTION: RATIOS

> **Tutorial note**. Although the question requires only two ratios to be calculated under each heading, for the benefit of students additional ratios are shown in the suggested solution below.

(a) Ratios which would be of interest to *shareholders* include the following.

		20X6	20X7
Earnings per share			
$\dfrac{\text{Profit after tax}}{\text{Number of shares}}$		£9,520 39,680	£11,660 39,680
	=	24p	29p
		20X6	*20X7*
ROCE			
$\dfrac{\text{Profit before interest and tax}}{\text{Capital employed}}$	=	17,238 60,580	20,670 69,840
	=	28.5%	29.6%
ROSC			
$\dfrac{\text{Profit before tax}}{\text{Shareholders' funds}}$	=	15,254 40,740	18,686 50,000
	=	37.4%	37.4%
Dividend cover			
$\dfrac{\text{Profit after tax}}{\text{Dividend payable}}$	=	9,520 2,240	11,660 2,400
	=	4.25	4.86

(b) Ratios relevant to *trade creditors* include the following.

Current ratio		20X6	20X7
$\dfrac{\text{Current assets}}{\text{Current liabilities}}$	=	92,447 36,862	99,615 42,275
	=	2.5	2.4

Acid test ratio			*20X6*	*20X7*
$\dfrac{\text{Current assets} - \text{stock}}{\text{Current liabilities}}$		=	$\dfrac{92{,}447 - 40{,}145}{36{,}862}$	$\dfrac{99{,}615 - 50{,}455}{42{,}475}$
		=	1.42	1.16

(c) Ratios relevant to *internal management* include the following.

Stock turnover (Assuming year end stock equates to average level)

$\dfrac{\text{Sales}}{\text{Average stock}}$	=	$\dfrac{486{,}300}{40{,}195}$	$\dfrac{583{,}900}{50{,}455}$
	=	12 times	11.6 times

Debtors collection period (assuming all sales are credit)

$\dfrac{\text{Debtors} \times 365}{\text{Sales}}$	=	$\dfrac{40{,}210 \times 365}{486{,}300}$	$\dfrac{43{,}370 \times 365}{583{,}900}$
	=	30.2 days	27.1 days

Gearing

$\dfrac{\text{Long-term debt}}{\text{Long-term debt} + \text{equity}}$	=	$\dfrac{19{,}840}{40{,}740 + 19{,}840}$	$\dfrac{19{,}840}{50{,}000 + 19{,}840}$
	=	32.7%	28.4%

44 PRACTICE QUESTION: RATIO JARGON

The bank manager's comments that the working capital ratio is too low while the gearing ratio is too high means that he considers that the company depends too heavily on outside finance.

The working capital ratio is the ratio of current assets to current liabilities. This ratio shows the extent to which a company's own funds have been used to finance the current assets as opposed to short-term borrowing. It is normally considered prudent to have a ratio of 2:1, with current assets covering current liabilities two-fold. However, companies frequently operate with a much lower working capital ratio, often nearer 1:1, but this still provides sufficient liquid funds to meet short-term liabilities. If this ratio falls too low, it means that the business relies too heavily on trade creditors or bank overdrafts to finance its activities, and could face difficulties in paying its bills, and short-term borrowings may be being used to fund fixed assets.

Gearing is a method of comparing how much of the long term capital of a business is provided by equity (ordinary shares and reserves) and how much is provided by investors who are entitled to a dividend or interest before ordinary shareholders can receive a dividend themselves. These sources of capital are preference shares or loans/debentures, which can be collectively referred to as prior charge capital. Gearing can be measured either as the ratio of prior charge capital to equity or to total long-term capital and neutral gearing would occur at 100% or 50% respectively (less than 100% representing 'low' gearing with the first method).

High gearing means that the prior charge capital exceeds the amount of equity and this can have advantages. By using debt capital, the interest or dividend is 'fixed' and diminishes in real terms in times of inflation, whereas ordinary shareholders expect growth. The return required by debt-holders is often lower than that expected by ordinary shareholders because their loans are normally secured on company assets whereas the ordinary shareholders' investment is subject to risk. High gearing benefits the ordinary shareholders when profits are high and the earnings per share increase.

High gearing can be an important factor when a company wants to raise extra capital. If gearing is high, would-be lenders may consider that the ordinary shareholders should provide a larger proportion of the company's capital. If they are not prepared to do so, this may imply that the company is considered to be a bad risk.

There is no specific level at which gearing is considered excessive and this can vary from company to company. Generally, the more stable the company, the 'safer' high gearing should be. If gearing appears to be too high, the company could experience difficulties in obtaining loans, which can lead to an increased cost of borrowing. Profits may not be sufficient to meet the interest charges, which are fixed, and provide a surplus for ordinary shareholders, further increasing the risk associated with investment in the company.

45 BIMBRIDGE

> **Tutorial note**. Do not be put off by the fact that you are writing to the managers of a hospitals trust – this is ratio analysis in its normal form. Don't forget – you need to *comment* on the ratios as well as calculating them correctly.

REPORT

To: The Managers, Bimbridge Hospitals Trust
From: A Technician
Date: 20 November 20X8

Performance and position of Patch Ltd

As requested, I have analysed the performance and position of Patch Ltd with special reference to selected accounting ratios. The calculation of the ratios is shown in the Appendix attached to this report. The purpose of the analysis is to determine whether we should use Patch Ltd as a supplier of bandages.

General comments

Both turnover and profits have increased over the two years. The company is clearly expanding, although not at an exceptionally fast rate. The growth seems to have been achieved without investing heavily in fixed assets, the fall in this figure presumably being due to depreciation. Shares were issued in 20X8 at a premium, while a sizeable portion of the long-term loan has been paid off. Expansion appears to be financed by share capital and profits.

Return on capital employed

This has increased from 8% in 20X7 to 10.3% in 20X8. It had also gone from being below the industry average in 20X7 to above it in 20X8. These are encouraging signs. As indicated above, the company has not invested significantly in fixed assets to finance its expansion – the assets/capital employed is simply working harder.

Net profit percentage

This has also increased from 22% in 20X7 to 24% in 20X8. In both years it was higher than the industry average. This is obviously good news. Sometimes when a company grows, it is at the expense of lower margins, but this is clearly not the case for Patch Ltd.

Quick ratio or acid test

The quick ratio shows how many assets, excluding stock, are available to meet the current liabilities. Stock is excluded because it is not always readily convertible into cash. The quick ratio or acid test is therefore a better indicator of a company's true liquidity than the current ratio which does not exclude stock. Patch Ltd's quick ratio is healthy (around 1) in both years, and has in fact improved from) 0.9:1 to 1.1:1. While Patch's quick ratio was the same as the industry average in 20X7, it was better than average in 20X8.

These are encouraging signs. Sometimes growth can lead to overtrading to the detriment of liquidity, but Patch Ltd has not fallen into this trap.

Gearing

The gearing ratio is also favourable. This can be calculated in two ways: debt/capital employed and debt/equity. Debt/capital employed shows a fall from 43% in 20X7 to 31% in 20X8. In 20X7 it was higher than the industry average, but in 20X8 it is lower. Calculated as debt/equity, the ratio shows an even more significant decline.

This is reassuring. A high geared company is more risky than a low geared one in that, if profits are falling, it is more difficult for a high geared company to meet interest payments. A high geared company is therefore more likely to go into liquidation, as our last supplier of bandages did.

Conclusion

On the basis of the above analysis, I see every reason to use Patch Ltd as our supplier. The company's profitability and liquidity are improving and the gearing is at a lower level than last year. In addition the company compares favourably with other companies operating in the same sector.

APPENDIX – CALCULATION OF RATIOS

	20X8	Industry average 20X8	20X7	Industry average 20X7
Return on capital employed	$\dfrac{552}{5,334} = 10.3\%$	9.6%	$\dfrac{462}{5,790} = 8.0\%$	9.4%
Net profit percentage	$\dfrac{552}{2,300} = 24\%$	21.4%	$\dfrac{462}{2,100} = 22\%$	21.3%
Quick ratio/acid test	$\dfrac{1,045 - 522}{475} = 1.1:1$	1.0:1	$\dfrac{837 - 419}{465} = 0.9:1$	0.9:1
Gearing: Debt/capital employed	$\dfrac{1,654}{5,334} = 31\%$	36%	$\dfrac{2,490}{5,790} = 43\%$	37%
Debt/equity	$\dfrac{1,654}{3,680} = 45\%$		$\dfrac{2,490}{3,300} = 75\%$	

46 BINS

REPORT

To: The Directors, Binns Ltd
From: A Technician
Date: 17 January 20X8
Subject: Financial statements of Gone Ltd

Introduction

The report analyses the financial statements of Gone Ltd with a view to assessing its suitability as a supplier for our company. The report shows certain key ratios covering profitability, liquidity and gearing. A comparison is made between 20X7 and 20X6 and also with the industry average for the year.

Summary of ratios

The ratios are summarised below. Calculations are shown in an appendix to this report.

	20X7	20X6
Return on capital employed	5.6%	11.1%
Gross profit percentage	39%	45%
Net profit percentage	11%	20.8%
Current ratio	1.2:1	2.1:1
Gearing	42.5%	20.5%

Profitability

Net profitability has declined in 20X7 in absolute terms as compared with 20X6 from £270,000 to £198,000, although gross profit has risen from £585,000 to £702,000. This is due to increased expenses - perhaps costs are not being kept under control. Turnover has increased. Possible an advertising campaign has been needed to expand the company's product range, although more information would be required to determine whether this is the case.

As regards profitability ratios, the 20X7 results show a decline as compared with 20X6. Return on capital employed and net profit margin are particularly worrying, having fallen by 50%. The 20X7 ratios for gross profit margin, net profit margin and return on capital employed are all below the industry average. In 20X6 the gross profit margin was above average, but this has now declined.

Overall the profitability figures are not particularly impressive. It is possible that some of this is due to the company's recent expansion - it has invested in fixed assets which have increased turnover but not profits as yet.

Liquidity

The current ratio is significantly worse in 20X7 than in 20X6 - 1.2 as opposed to 2.1. It is also much less in 20X7 than the industry average, whereas in 20X6 it was higher. This is a cause for concern, although the information does not show the components of current assets. If the fall is due to reduced stock levels, this is less of a worry than a lower bank balance.

Gearing

As we are considering Gone Ltd as a potential supplier, we should be very wary of any factors which suggest that it may not be able to continue in business. High gearing is one such factor. Large debts carry risk of insolvency, and the company may have difficulty meeting interest payments.

The level of gearing has doubled in 20X7 and has gone from being comfortably below the industry average to worryingly above it. This, more than profitability or liquidity should be of concern to us. The company has used debt finance rather than equity to expand its fixed asset base, but has not as yet increased profits.

Conclusion

On the basis of the above analysis, particularly as regards the level of gearing, I would recommend that we use an alternative supplier. It is possible that Gone Ltd's investment in fixed assets will lead to a successful expansion of the business in the future, in which case we should reconsider our decision.

APPENDIX: CALCULATION OF RATIOS

	20X7	*20X6*
Return on capital employed	$\dfrac{198}{2,034 + 1,506} = 5.6\%$	$\dfrac{270}{1,938 + 500} = 11.1\%$
Gross profit percentage	$\dfrac{702}{1,800} = 39\%$	$\dfrac{585}{1,300} = 45\%$
Net profit percentage	$\dfrac{198}{1,800} = 11\%$	$\dfrac{270}{1,300} = 20.8\%$
Current ratio	$\dfrac{460}{383} = 1.2{:}1$	$\dfrac{853}{406} = 2.1{:}1$
Gearing	$\dfrac{1,506}{2,034 + 1,506} = 42.5\%$	$\dfrac{500}{1,938 + 500} = 20.5\%$

47 ANIMALETS

> **Tutorial note**. As well as being a straightforward ratio analysis and cash flow reconciliation, this question also tests whether you have a good understanding of the status of investments in the context of consolidation.

(a)

REPORT

To: The Directors, Animalets plc
From: A Technician
Date: 20 November 20X8

Performance and position of Superpet Ltd

As requested, I have analysed the performance and position of Superpet Ltd with special reference to selected accounting ratios. The calculation of the ratios is shown in the Appendix attached to this report.

General

Superpet is clearly expanding; both turnover and profit are up on 20X7. The company has invested in new fixed assets by increasing borrowing and issuing share capital.

Gross profit ratio

This has increased slightly from 53% in 20X7 to 58% in 20X8. This is due to a large increase in turnover and the fact that the cost of sales has not increased in proportion to the sales. Clearly, then, the company is not achieving increased sales at the expense of lower margins.

Current ratio

The current ratio has fallen slightly, but not significantly. It is still reasonably healthy. Sometimes expansion can give rise to overtrading, but this has not happened with Superpet.

Acid test ratio

This ratio, because it excludes stock, may be regarded as a better indicator of the company's liquidity than the current ratio. Despite Superpet's expansion, the acid test ratio is healthy and shows a slight improvement on the previous year.

Gearing ratio

As mentioned above, Superpet has had to finance expansion by raising capital. Encouragingly, although the loan has increased, the gearing ratio, which was very low, has fallen. This is because there has been a proportionally greater increase in the capital and reserves.

Conclusion

Overall, Superpet Ltd is expanding and healthy and the ratios do not give any cause for concern.

APPENDIX – CALCULATION OF RATIOS

	20X8	20X7
Gross profit	$\dfrac{1{,}150}{2{,}000} = 58\%$	$\dfrac{800}{1{,}500} = 53\%$

Current ratio

$\dfrac{\text{Current assets}}{\text{Current liabilities}}$	$\dfrac{870}{670} = 1.3$	$\dfrac{610}{448} = 1.4$

Acid test ratio

$\dfrac{\text{Current assets less stock}}{\text{Current liabilities}}$	$\dfrac{(870 - 350)}{670} = 0.8$	$\dfrac{(610 - 300)}{448} = 0.7$

Gearing ratio

$\dfrac{\text{Long-term loan}}{\text{Long-term loan + capital \& reserves}}$	$\dfrac{100}{1{,}338} = 7\%$	$\dfrac{70}{800} = 9\%$

or

$\dfrac{\text{Long-term loan}}{\text{Capital \& reserves}}$	$\dfrac{100}{1{,}238} = 8\%$	$\dfrac{70}{730} = 10\%$

(b) SUPERPET LIMITED
RECONCILIATION OF OPERATING PROFIT
TO NET CASH INFLOW FROM OPERATING ACTIVITIES

	£'000
Operating profit	958
Depreciation	65
Profit on sale of asset	(5)
Increase in stocks	(50)
Increase in debtors	(150)
Increase in creditors	42
	860

(c) (i) If Animalets were to purchase 30% of the shares of Superpet, giving the directors significant influence over Superpet, the latter would be an *associate* of Animalets. The accounting treatment would then follow FRS 9 and is known as *equity accounting*.

Consolidated profit and loss account

(1) Animalets' share of the operating profit of Superpet should be included immediately after group operating results.

(2) From the level of profit before tax, Animalets' share of the relevant amounts of Superpet should be included within amounts for the group.

(3) Group share of Superpet's tax should be disclosed in a note.

Consolidated balance sheet

(1) Group share of net assets of Superpet should be disclosed.

(2) Goodwill on acquisition, less any amortisation should be disclosed separately.

(ii) If Animalets were to purchase a 75% stake, together with dominant influence, Superpet would be a *subsidiary* of Animalets. In the consolidated accounts, the income and expenditure and the assets and liabilities of Superpet would be added on a line-by-line basis to those of Animalets under *acquisition accounting*. The remaining 25% of the shares not acquired by Animalets would be shown as a minority interest.

48 PRACTICE QUESTION: CONSOLIDATED FINANCIAL STATEMENTS

> **Tutorial note**. Answers to this type of question must be well-structured and argued logically; avoid rambling answers.

The individual accounts of a parent company are inadequate by themselves for the information needs of shareholders and other interested parties.

(a) The parent company accounts do not reveal the true size and importance of the economic entity in which shareholders have invested.

(b) They show investments in subsidiaries at historical cost, which may be a very poor indication of the resources actually controlled by the group.

(c) Parent company profit will consist only of its own operating profit, other investment income and so on and dividends received from subsidiaries. Shareholders will not know the amount of profits retained by subsidiaries.

(d) Creditors cannot assess, from the parent company accounts alone, the liquidity and solvency of the group as a whole.

The preparation of group accounts helps to overcome these difficulties and therefore provides fuller information than would be available from the parent company accounts. The statement in the question cannot be strictly justified: since individual accounts must still be prepared for each group company, the consolidated accounts are an *additional* source of information which can only be helpful to accounts users.

However, it is true that group accounts taken by themselves suffer from serious shortcomings.

(a) They conceal the liquidity and solvency position of individual group companies. Similarly, the losses of some group companies may be concealed by the overall profitability of the group.

(b) They aggregate assets which may be very disparate in nature.

(c) The do not reveal the extent of intra-group trading and intra-group indebtedness.

(d) They are unsuitable for detailed ratio analysis because they do not indicate which sectors of the group's activities are generating a high level of return and which are less satisfactory.

Some of these objections have been reduced in recent years by statutory provisions on the disclosure of segmental information, but the Companies Act 1985 does not go very far in this direction. SSAP 25 *Segmental reporting* has increased the amount of information to be disclosed in this way although the basis of inter-segmental pricing need not be disclosed.

49 BATH

> **Tutorial note**. This question introduces the complication of dividends proposed by the subsidiaries but not yet accrued for by Bath Ltd. Notice that the profit and loss working must therefore include the proposed dividends.

BATH LIMITED
CONSOLIDATED BALANCE SHEET AS AT 31 DECEMBER 20X1

	£	£
Fixed assets		
Intangible assets		
Goodwill arising on consolidation (W1)		164,160
Tangible assets		
Freehold property at NBV	267,000	
Plant and machinery at NBV	395,800	
		662,800
Investment		52,000
		878,960
Current assets		
Stocks and work in progress (W3)	598,560	
Debtors	340,200	
Cash at bank and in hand	73,700	
	1,012,460	
Creditors: amounts falling due		
within one year		
Bank overdraft	72,300	
Trade creditors	385,400	
Proposed dividend	30,000	
Other creditors (W4)	170,600	
	658,300	
Net current assets		354,160
Total assets less current liabilities		1,233,120
Minority interests (W5)		258,880
		974,240
Share capital and reserves		
Called up share capital		750,000
Share premium account		15,000
Profit and loss account (W6)		209,240
		974,240

Workings

1   *Goodwill*

	Jankin		Arthur	
	£	£	£	£
Cost of investment		153,000		504,000
Less dividend paid from				
pre-acquisition profits				
$(24,000 \times {}^{6}/_{12} \times 60\%)$		-		(7,200)
		153,000		496,800
Net assets acquired				
Share capital	100,000		400,000	
Reserves at acquisition (W2)	19,400		159,000	
	119,400		559,000	
Group share	@ 80%	95,520	@ 60%	335,400
		57,480		161,400
Amortisation at 25%		(14,370)		(40,350)
CBS		43,110		121,050

2 *Reserves at acquisition*

	£
Arthur	
Retained profits brought forward	132,000
To 30 June 20X1 (54,000 × $^6/_{12}$)	27,000
	159,000
Jankin	
Retained profits brought forward	19,400
(no adjustment required as acquired at beginning of year)	

3 *Stocks and work in progress*

		£
Per question:	Bath	206,000
	Jankin	99,000
	Arthur	294,200
		599,200
Add stock in transit (at cost to group)		960
Less profit in stock held by Jankin		(1,600)
Stocks in consolidated balance sheet		598,560

4 *Other creditors*

	£	£
Taxation		158,000
Dividends payable to minorities		
Jankin (20% × £15,000)	3,000	
Arthur (40% × £24,000)	9,600	
		12,600
		170,600

5 *Minority interests*

	Jankin £	Arthur £
Share capital	100,000	400,000
Reserves	22,400	186,000
	122,400	586,000
MI	20%	40%
	24,480	234,400

CBS = £(234,400 + 24,480) = £258,880

6 *Profit and loss account*

	£
Bath Ltd	228,000
Add: dividend from Jankin (£15,000 × 80%)	12,000
post-acquisition dividend from Arthur (£24,000 × 60% × $^6/_{12}$)	7,200
	247,200
Jankin: group share of post acquisition retained reserves (£3,000 × 80%)	2,400
Arthur: group share of post acquisition retained reserves (£186,000 – £159,000) × 60%	16,200
Unrealised profit	(1,840)
Goodwill amortised (W1)	(54,720)
CBS	209,240

50 THOMAS

THOMAS LIMITED
CONSOLIDATED BALANCE SHEET AS AT 30 SEPTEMBER 20X6

	£'000	£'000
Fixed assets		640
Intangible: goodwill		16,932
Current tangible assets		
Stocks	8,702	
Debtors	6,378	
Cash	331	
	15,411	
Current liabilities		
Trade creditors	4,494	
Taxation	1,007	
	5,501	
Net current assets		9,910
Total assets less current liabilities		27,482
Long-term loan		9,500
		17,982
Capital and reserves		
Called up share capital		5,000
Share premium		2,500
Profit and loss account		9,550
		17,050
Minority interest		932
		17,982

Workings

1   *Group structure*

Thomas Ltd
|
$\dfrac{800,000}{1,000,000}$ 80%
|
James Ltd

2   *Goodwill*

	£'000	£'000
Cost of investment		3,760
Net assets acquired		
Share capital	1,000	
Share premium	400	
Revaluation reserve (3,910 – 3,410)	500	
Profit and loss account	2,000	
	3,900	
Group share × 80%		3,120
Goodwill		640

3   *Minority interest*

	£'000
Net assets at 30 September 20X6	
Share capital	1,000
Share premium	400
Revaluation reserve	500
Profit and loss account	2,760
	4,660

Minority interest = £4,660,000 × 20% = £932,000.

4   *Profit and loss account*

	£'000
Thomas Ltd	8,942
James Ltd 80% × (2,760 – 2,000)	608
	9,550

51   ENTERPRISE AND VULCAN

Step 1

Calculate the goodwill in the investment in Vulcan Ltd. This will be needed in order to calculate the 'Investment in associated undertakings' line on the balance sheet since goodwill is being amortised, and is not yet fully amortised.

Goodwill

	£'000	£'000
Cost of investment		2,000
Share capital	2,000	
Revaluation reserve	200	
Profit and loss reserve	900	
	3,100	
× 30%		(930)
		1,070

£1,070,000 ÷ 5 = 214,000 amortised per year

3 years amortised already £214,000 × = 642,000

Add this year's amortisation of £214,000:

£	
856,000	amortised to date
214,000	Unamortised
1,070,000	total goodwill

Step 2

Complete the top half of the balance sheet including the 'Investments in associates' line as below, and insert the share capital of Enterprise plc.

	£'000
Investment in associate's net assets	
(30% × 7,940,000)	2,382
Unamortised goodwill (see Step 1))	214
	2,596

Step 3

Calculate the balance sheet reserves.

1   *Revaluation reserve*

	£'000	£'000
Enterprise plc		2,000
Vulcan Ltd: at balance sheet	1,000	
at acquisition	(200)	
	800	
× 30%		240
		2,240

2   *Profit and loss reserve*

	£	£
Enterprise plc		5,100
Vulcan Ltd: at balance sheet	4,940	
at acquisition	(900)	
	4,040	
	× 30%	1,212
Less goodwill amortised to date (see Step 1)		(856)
		5,456

Step 4

Complete the consolidated P&L account up to the group operating profit line, and calculate the share of operating profit in the associate. Any adjustments to the P&L account for the amortisation of goodwill should be charged now to reduce this figure.

Share of operating profit in associate

	£'000
Operating profit × 30% (£2,120,000 × 30%)	636
Amortisation for the year (see task one)	(214)
	422

Step 5

Complete the balance sheet and profit and loss account.

ENTERPRISE PLC
CONSOLIDATED BALANCE SHEET AS AT 30 JUNE 20X8

	£'000	£'000
Fixed assets		
Tangible assets		8,000
Investments:		
Investments in associates		2,596
		10,596
Current assets		
Stock	1,340	
Debtors	1,000	
Cash	260	
	2,600	
Creditors (due within one year)	(1,500)	
Net current assets		1,100
		11,696

ENTERPRISE PLC GROUP
CONSOLIDATED PROFIT AND LOSS ACCOUNT
FOR THE YEAR ENDING 30 JUNE 20X8

	£'000	£'000
Group turnover		10,000
Cost of sales		(6,000)
Gross profit		4,000
Expenses		(1,500)
Group operating profit		2,500
Share of operating profit in associates	636	
Amortisation in associate	(214)	
		422
		2,922
Interest payable:		
Group		(100)
Associates (30% × 20,000)		(6)
Profit on ordinary activities before tax		2,816
Tax on profit on ordinary activities★		(1,010)
Profit on ordinary activities after tax		1,806
Equity dividends		(600)
Retained profit for the group and its share of associates		1,206

★ Tax relates to the following:

Parent and subsidiaries	£800,000
Associates (30% × £700,000)	£210,000

Note: As the share in the associates is equal to more than 25% of the group figure (before associates) for operating profit, additional disclosures required under FRS 9 would need to be given, if not specifically excluded from the question requirements.

52   SCENARIO: PAPIER MÂCHÉ

SECTION 1

Task 1.1

REPORT

To: The Directors
       Machier Ltd
From: A Technician
Date: 20 April 20X9

Financial Statements of Machier Ltd

This report analyses the financial statements of Machier Ltd, commenting the company's profitability, liquidity and financial position. It also assesses whether or not it is likely that the bank will give the company a loan based on the financial statements.

My analysis uses key accounting ratios, calculations of which are contained in an appendix to this report. It discusses changes which have taken place between 20X8 and 20X9.

Comment and analysis

In absolute terms, turnover and profits have both increased from 20X8 to 20X9. The company appears to be expanding, and has invested heavily in fixed assets in order to do so. However, when we look at the ratios, the picture is less favourable.

Return on equity has fallen from 21.7% to 18.8%. Operating profit as a percentage of turnover has gone down from 31% to 28%, but when interest payments are taken into account, the fall is more dramatic, from 24% to 18%. This is because, in 20X9, the company is servicing a much bigger loan.

The liquidity position has deteriorated. The obvious change is cash – the company has gone from a positive bank balance of £86,000 to a bank overdraft of £183,000. This deterioration is reflected in the liquidity ratios. The quick ratio or acid test has fallen from 1.2:1 in 20X8, when there were more than enough quick assets to cover current liabilities, to 0.7:1 in 20X9 when there are not enough. The quick ratio excludes stock, as stock is less liquid than other current assets. Stocks have risen over the period – but how easily could they be sold to raise cash?

The company has borrowed much more money in 20X9 – the long-term loan has almost doubled compared with 20X8. The loan has probably been used to invest in fixed assets so that the business can expand. Interest payments are still easily covered by profits, although interest cover has declined from 4.4 times to 2.9 times. However, the effect of increased borrowing on the company's gearing ratio is a matter of concern. The debt/equity ratio has increased from 122% to 164%, and the capital gearing ratio from 55% to 62%. Highly geared companies are more risky – if profits were to decline, would the company be able to meet interest payments?

Conclusion

Based on the two years' financial statements, the bank may be reluctant to give the company a loan. Although turnover and profits are increasing, profitability ratios are declining. The bank may also be concerned about liquidity, particularly the cash position. Above all, the bank may well be reluctant to lend to a company which is already highly geared.

You may like to consider alternative ways of financing expansion, for example issuing more equity shares. This would have the effect of reducing gearing.

I hope this report gives you the information you require in order to make a decision.

Signed: A Technician

APPENDIX: CALCULATION OF RATIOS

Ratio	*20X9*	*20X8*
Return on equity		
$\dfrac{\text{Profit after tax}}{\text{Share capital \& reserves}}$	$\dfrac{321}{1,708} = 18.8\%$	$\dfrac{266}{1,227} = 21.7\%$
Net profit percentage		
$\dfrac{\text{Operating profit}}{\text{Turnover}}$	$\dfrac{738}{2,636} = 28\%$	$\dfrac{523}{1,687} = 31\%$
Or: $\dfrac{\text{Profit before tax}}{\text{Turnover}}$	$\dfrac{486}{2,636} = 18\%$	$\dfrac{403}{1,687} = 24\%$
Quick ratio/acid test		
$\dfrac{\text{Current assets less stock}}{\text{Current liabilities}}$	$\dfrac{527}{749} = 0.7:1$	$\dfrac{423}{359} 1.2:1$
Gearing ratio		
$\dfrac{\text{Debt}}{\text{Equity}}$	$\dfrac{2,800}{1,708} = 164\%$	$\dfrac{1,500}{1,227+1,500} = 55\%$
Or: $\dfrac{\text{Debt}}{\text{Total capital}}$	$\dfrac{2,800}{1,708+2,800} 62\%$	$\dfrac{1,500}{1,227} = 122\%$
Interest cover		
$\dfrac{\text{Profit before interest \& tax}}{\text{Interest paid}}$	$\dfrac{738}{252} = 2.9 \text{ times}$	$\dfrac{523}{120} = 4.4 \text{ times}$

Task 1.2

NOTES FOR THE DIRECTORS

(a) *Elements of a balance sheet*

The elements of a balance sheet are identified in the ASB's *Statement of Principles*. They are assets, liabilities and ownership interest. The balance sheet of Machier Ltd can be analysed as follows.

Element	*Balances*
Assets	Fixed assets
	Current assets
Liabilities	Current liabilities
	Long-term loan
Ownership interest	Capital and reserves

(b) The accounting equation is:

Assets LESS liabilities = Ownership interest

This can be applied to Machier Ltd as follows.

Assets	LESS	Liabilities	=	Ownership interest
£4,282 +£975=		£749+£2,800		£1,708
£5,257		= £3,549		

(c) By definition, a not-for-profit organisation does not exist to make a profit, so a profit and loss account would not be appropriate. Instead, an income and expenditure account would be used. This is similar in many ways to the profit and loss account – income is matched against expenditure used in generating the income to arrive at a surplus or deficit. The surplus is equivalent to a profit and the deficit is equivalent to a loss.

(d) The 'capital' of a not-for-profit organisation is the balance on its accumulated fund(s). Such funds can be given many names and are used for the purposes of the organisation. Any surplus or deficit on the income and expenditure account is transferred to the accumulated fund at the end of the accounting period.

(e) The financial statements of a profit-making organisation, such as a commercial company are as defined in the ASB's *Statement of Principles,* that is 'to provide information about the financial position, performance and financial adaptability of an enterprise that is useful to a wide range of users for assessing the stewardship of management and for making economic decisions'.

A company's financial statements reflect the fact that the managers are accountable, principally to the investors or shareholders, for whom the company exists primarily to make a profit. But not-for-profit organisations exist not to make a profit but to provide a service. So their financial statements should show whether the service has been provided in an efficient and appropriate manner. Here are some examples.

(i) A *charity's* financial statements should be aimed at *donors* and should show whether their donations have been put to good use.

(ii)   A *club's accounts* should show the *members* whether their subscription money has been put to good use, and whether the club has been run in accordance with its regulations and aims.

(iii) *Local authority financial statements* should show *council tax payers* whether the local authority has given value for money.

(iv)   The accounts of *NHS trusts* should indicate to the *Department of Health* whether the trust has been efficiently run by the managers.

SECTION 2

Part A

Task 2.1

MACHIER LIMITED
RECONCILATION OF OPERATING PROFIT
TO NET CASH INFLOW FROM OPERATING ACTIVITIES

	£'000
Operating profit	738
Add back depreciation	856
Less profit on sale of tangible fixed asset	(7)
Increase in stock (448 – 287)	(161)
Increase in debtors (527 – 337)	(190)
Increase in creditors (381 – 212)	169
	1,405

Task 2.2

MACHIER LIMITED
CASH FLOW STATEMENT FOR THE YEAR ENDED 31 MARCH 20X9

	£'000	£'000
Net cash inflow from operating activities		1,405
Returns on investments and servicing of finance		
Interest paid		(252)
Taxation		(137)
Capital expenditure		
Payments to acquire fixed assets (W1)	(2,771)	
Receipts from sale of fixed assets (W2)	16	
		(2,755)
		(1,739)
Equity dividends paid (W3)		(30)
Net cash outflow before financing		(1,769)
Financing		
Loan	1,300	
Issue of shares	200	
		1,500
Decrease in cash		269

Workings

1   *Purchase of fixed assets*

FIXED ASSETS

	£'000		£'000
Balance b/d	2,376	Disposals (NBV) (28 – 19)	9
Additions	2,771	Depreciation	856
(Bal. fig)		Balance c/d	4,282
	5,147		5,147

2   *Sale of fixed asset*

	£'000
Profit on sale	7
NBV	9
∴ Proceeds	16

3   *Dividends*

DIVIDENDS

	£'000		£'000
∴ Cash (Bal. fig.)	30	Balance b/d	10
Balance c/d	20	P & L	40
	50		50

Task 2.3

	£'000	£'000
Cost of investment		1,761
Share of net assets acquired		
Share capital	200	
Share premium	100	
Revaluation reserve (4,682 – 4,282)	400	
Profit and loss account	1,408	
	2,108	
Group share 75%		1,581
Goodwill		180

Task 2.4

NOTE TO THE DIRECTORS – TREATMENT OF GOODWILL

(a) Both positive purchased goodwill and purchased intangible assets should initially be capitalised and classed as an asset at cost.

(b) Inherent (non-purchased) goodwill should not be capitalised.

(c) When intangible assets are acquired as part of a takeover they should be capitalised separately from goodwill if their fair value can be reliably measured. If this is not possible, then they should be subsumed into goodwill.

(d) If, after stringently testing the fair values of the assets for impairment, negative goodwill arises this should be shown on the balance sheet separately and immediately below positive goodwill.

(e) Goodwill and intangible assets should be amortised on a systematic basis over their useful economic lives. If it is considered that the economic life is infinite no amortisation is needed.

(f) It is presumed that intangibles (including goodwill) have a life of less than 20 years but this is rebuttable. This, however, puts the responsibility on the reporting entity to demonstrate that not only does the asset have an extended life but that its value is capable of an annual impairment review.

(g)   In all cases the economic life should be reviewed annually.

Part B

Task 2.5

> **Tutorial note**. Remember to take into account the adjustments to the retained profit given in the ETB. Investments could also be shown under current assets.

TYPESET LIMITED
BALANCE SHEET AS AT 31 MARCH 20X9

	£'000	£'000
Fixed assets		
Tangible assets (W1)		5,820
Investments		1,580
		7,400
Current assets		
Stocks	4,187	
Debtors (W2)	3,153	
Cash at bank and in hand	216	
	7,556	
Creditors: amounts falling due within one year (W4)	2,728	
Net current assets		4,828
Total assets less current liabilities		12,228
Creditors: amounts falling due after one year		
Long-term loan		1,450
		10,778
Capital and reserves		
Called up share capital		5,000
Share premium		1,200
Revaluation reserve		500
Profit and loss account (W5)		4,078
		10,778

Workings

1   *Tangible assets*

	Cost	Acc. Depn.	NBV
	£'000	£'000	£'000
Land	2,075	-	2,075
Buildings	2,077	383	1,694
Fixtures and fittings	1,058	495	563
Motor vehicles	2,344	1,237	1,107
Office equipment	533	152	381
	8,087	2,267	5,820

2   *Debtors*

	£'000
Trade debtors per trial balance	3,136
Less provision for doubtful debts (W3)	80
	3,056
Prepayments	97
	3,153

3   *Provision for doubtful debts*

	£'000
Debtors per trial balance	3,136
Less doubtful debt	36
	3,100
Provision for doubtful debt:	
3,100 × 2%	62
Add 50% of doubtful debt	18
Total provision	80
Existing provision	37
∴ Increase in provision	43

4   *Creditors*: amounts falling due within one year

	£'000
Trade creditors	1,763
Corporation tax payable	493
Dividends payable	350
Accruals	122
	2,728

5   *Profit and loss account*

	£'000
At 1 April 20X8	3,533
Retained profit for the year (W6)	545
At 31 March 20X9	4,078

6   *Retained profit for the year*

	£'000
Retained profit per trial balance	1,431
Dividend payable	(350)
Corporation tax	(493)
Increase in doubtful debt provision	(43)
	545

DECEMBER 1999 CENTRAL ASSESSMENT: ANSWERS

SECTION 1

Part A

Task 1.1

> **Tutorial note.** You could have chosen examples other than the ones we discuss here.

(a) *Assessing the stewardship of management*

An example of an external user of the financial statements of a profit-making organisation is a shareholder in a limited company.

He or she would assess management's stewardship by looking at the return on net assets, or the return on equity. He might also be interested in the cash position.

As regards the not-for-profit sector, management's stewardship might be assessed in a number of ways.

(i) People making donations to a charity would want to see that those donations have been used effectively.

(ii) Council tax payers will want to know whether the local authority has given value for money.

(iii) Club members will want to see that their subscriptions have been put to good use in the running of the club.

(iv) Trustees of NHS trusts will want to know whether the managers have given value for money.

(b) *Making economic decisions*

In the profit-making sector, the financial statements of a limited company could be used by a potential investor to help him decide whether to buy shares in the company. The financial statements of a partnership might help a bank decide whether to lend money to the partnership.

The financial statements of a non-profit making organisation such as a local authority could by a potential supplier of goods or services.

Part B

Task 1.2

(a) A balance sheet is a list of all the assets owned by a business and all the liabilities owed by a business as at a particular date. It is a snapshot of the financial position of the business at a particular moment.

The profit and loss account is a record of income generated and expenditure incurred over a given period. It shows whether the business has had more income than expenditure (a profit) or vice versa (a loss). It can also be viewed as the difference between the opening and closing balance sheets.

(b)   The accounting equation is:

ASSETS LESS LIABILITIES = CAPITAL (OWNERSHIP INTEREST)

Applying that to the financial statements of Carp Ltd (all figures £'000):

ASSETS	LESS	LIABILITIES	=	CAPITAL
4,214 + 1,341 = 5.555		838 + 2,500 = 3,338		2,217

(c)   Calculation of ratios

		1999		1998	
(i)	*Gearing*				
	$\dfrac{\text{Debt}}{\text{Capital employed}}$	$\dfrac{2,500}{4,717}$ = 53%		$\dfrac{1,000}{2,703}$ = 37%	
	OR $\dfrac{\text{Debt}}{\text{Equity}}$	$\dfrac{2,500}{2,217}$ = 113%		$\dfrac{1,000}{1,703}$ = 59%	
(ii)	*Net profit percentage*				
	$\dfrac{\text{Net profit before interest and tax}}{\text{Sales}}$	$\dfrac{668}{3,183}$ = 21%		$\dfrac{689}{2,756}$ = 25%	
(iii)	*Current ratio*				
	$\dfrac{\text{Current assets}}{\text{Current liabilities}}$	$\dfrac{1,341}{838}$ = 1.6:1		$\dfrac{1,284}{611}$ = 2.1:1	
(iv)	*Return on equity*				
	$\dfrac{\text{Profit after tax}}{\text{Capital and reserves}}$	$\dfrac{356}{2,217}$ = 16%		$\dfrac{471}{1,703}$ = 28%	

(d)   (i)   *Gearing ratio*

This has increased considerably between 1998 and 1999, whether measured as debt to capital employed or debt to equity. The obvious reason for this is that the long-term loan has almost doubled. There is a risk in a highly geared company that interest payments may not be met if profits fall.

(ii)   *Net profit percentage*

This ratio has fallen from 25% to 21%. Net profit has remained almost static, despite an increase in turnover and gross profit. Perhaps expenses need to be monitored.

(iii)   *Current ratio*

The current ratio has fallen during the year, which means that there are fewer current assets to cover current liabilities. This is of particular concern when you see that a large part of current assets consists of stock, which is less liquid than debtors or cash.

(iv)   *Return on equity*

This has fallen to just under half what it was in 1998. Return on equity is a measure of management's stewardship and should be a matter of concern to potential investors. Basically, the company is not making as much profit from the equity invested as it did last year.

Overall, the financial position of the company has deteriorated showing adverse trends in all the types of ratio.

(e)   Taking into account the deterioration in profitability, liquidity and gearing shown in the ratios calculated above, the company is a worse prospect for investment in 1999 than it was in 1998.

SECTION 2

Part A

Task 2.1

> **Tutorial note**. The accumulated profits of Hower Ltd are not included in consolidated reserves as they are pre-acquisition.

SHOPAN GROUP
CONSOLIDATED BALANCE SHEET AS AT 30 SEPTEMBER 1999

	£'000	£'000
Fixed assets		
Tangible assets		8,306
Goodwill		222
Current assets		
Stocks (1,902 + 865)	2,766	
Debtors (1,555 + 547)	2,102	
Cash (184 + 104)	288	
	5,156	
Current liabilities		
Trade creditors (1,516 + 457)	1,973	
Taxation (431 + 188)	619	
	2,592	
Net current assets		2,564
Total assets less current liabilities		11,092
Long-term loan (2870 + 400)		(3,270)
		7,822
Capital and reserves		
Called up share capital		2,000
Share premium		950
Profit and loss account		4,246
		7,196
Minority interests		626
		7,822

Workings

1 *Group Structure*

Shopan
75%
Hower

2 *Goodwill*

	£'000	£'000
Cost		2,100
Net assets acquired		
Share capital	500	
Share premium	120	
Profit and loss	1,484	
Revaluation reserve	400	
(2,033 – 1,633)	2,504	
Group share 75%		1,878
Goodwill		222

3   *Minority interest*

Net assets acquired (W2): £2,504,000

Minority interests: 2,504 × 25% = 626

4   *Fixed assets*

	£'000
Shopan	6,273
Hower	1,633
Revaluation	400
	8,306

Task 2.2

An undertaking (H) is the parent of its subsidiary undertaking (S) if any of the following criteria apply.

(a) H is a member of S and either holds or controls more than 50% of the voting rights or controls the board.

(b) S is a subsidiary because it is a subsidiary of a subsidiary of H, ie S is a sub-subsidiary.

(c) H has the right to exercise a dominant influence over S (laid down in the memorandum or articles or a control contract.

(d) H has a participating interest in S and either actually exercises a dominant influence over S or H and S are managed on a unified basis.

Part B

Task 2.3

DIEWELT LIMITED
CASH FLOW STATEMENT FOR THE YEAR ENDED 30 SEPTEMBER 1999

	£'000	£'000
Net cash inflow from operating activities		1,242
Returns on investments and servicing of finance		
Interest paid	365	
Taxation	491	
Capital expenditure		(856)
Payments to acquire tangible fixed assets (W1)	(1,906)	
Receipts from sale of fixed assets (W2)	108	
		(1,798)
		(1,412)
Equity dividends paid (W3)		(368)
Net cash outflow before financing		(1,780)
Financing		
Increase in loan (3,300 – 2,900)	400	
Issue of ordinary share capital (2,200 – 1,600)	600	
Share premium (800 – 300)	500	
		1,500
Decrease in cash		(280)

Workings

1 *Payments to acquire tangible fixed assets*

FIXED ASSETS

	£'000		£'000
Balance b/d	5,620	NBV of assets sold (136 – 85)	51
Additions (bal. figure)	1,906	Depreciation	985
	7,526	Balance c/d	6,490
			7,526

2 *Receipts from sale of fixed assets*

	£'000
Profit	57
Net book value	51
Proceeds	108

3 *Dividends*

DIVIDENDS

	£'000		£'000
Cash paid (bal. fig.)	368	Balance b/f	192
Bal. c/f	264	P & L	440
	632		632

Part C

Task 2.4

			£'000	£'000
(a)	DEBIT	Stock - balance sheet	46,077 (W1)	
	CREDIT	Stock - profit and loss account		46,077
(b)	DEBIT	Prepayments	1,200	
	CREDIT	Rent, rates and insurance		1,200
(c)	DEBIT	Drawings	2,000	
	CREDIT	Purchases		2,000
(d)	DEBIT	Depreciation (motor vehicles)	5,292	
	CREDIT	Motor vehicles – accumulated depreciation (W2)		5,292

Workings

1 *Stock*

Write down to NRV = £8,200 – £4,800
= £3,400
∴ Value of closing stock = £49,477 – £3,400
= £46,077

2 *Motor vehicles depreciation*

NBV = £36,000 – £18,360 = £17,640
∴ Depreciation = £17,640 × 30%
= £5,292

Task 2.5

ELIZABETH OGIER
PROFIT AND LOSS ACCOUNT FOR THE YEAR ENDED 30 SEPTEMBER 1999

	£'000	£'000
Sales		230,461
Less returns inwards		3,053
		227,408
Cost of sales (W1)		109,925
Gross profit		117,483
Less expenses		
Rent, rates and insurance (8,291 – 1,200)	7,091	
Motor expenses	5,813	
Bad debts	1,420	
Carriage outwards	1,571	
Salesperson's commission	2,561	
Bank charges	710	
Depreciation: office equipment	2,312	
fixtures and fittings	602	
Motor vehicles	5,292	
Wages, salaries and NIC	47,564	
Lighting and heating	3,056	
Postage and stationery	1,037	
Telephone	3,571	
Discounts allowed	410	
		83,010
Net profit		34,473

Workings

1   *Cost of sales*

	£'000
Opening stock	46,092
Purchases (113,565 – 2,000)	111,565
Carriage inwards	1,256
Returns outwards	(2,911)
	156,002
Less closing stock	46,077
	109,925

Task 2.6

A Technician
ABC Accountants
12 Bradshaw Rd
Bolton
BL2 1RJ

Ms E Ogier
Magnifique Perfumes
1 Moor Lane
Bolton
BL4 6GF

3 November 1999

I am writing to explain why I have made adjustments to certain figures in your trial balance before preparing the final accounts.

Stock valuation on 30 September 1999

The valuation of closing stock had to be adjusted because the original figure of £49,477 contained some goods which had cost £8,200, but which could now be sold for only £4,800. The adjustment has to be made because the relevant accounting standard, SSAP 9 *Stocks and long-term contracts* requires that stocks should be valued at *the lower of cost and net realisable value.* Cost here is higher than net realisable value, so the stocks must be written down to net realisable value of £4,800. The total value of stock must be adjusted by the amount of the write down (£3,400) giving a value of £46,077.

Goods taken for personal use

This adjustment was made because of the *business entity concept,* which states that a business is a separate entity from its owners. The goods were taken for personal use, and should not, therefore be treated as an expense of the business. They are in fact drawings from the business, that is a reduction in business capital. Purchases should therefore be reduced (a credit) and the value of the goods should be debited to drawings.

If you wish to discuss these adjustments further, please do not hesitate to contact me.

Yours sincerely

A Technician

Part D

Task 2.7

> **Tutorial note**. Drawings were given to you as a 'red herring'. They do not come into the appropriation account.

GEOFFREY, VICTORIA AND ALBERTINE
APPROPRIATION ACCOUNT FOR THE YEAR ENDED 30 SEPTEMBER 1999

	£'000	£'000
Net profit for year		115,960
Less partners' salaries		
Geoffrey	25,000	
Victoria	19,000	
Albertine	15,000	
		(59,000)
Less interest on capital		
Geoffrey (8% × 56,000)	4,480	
Victoria (8% × 23,000)	1,840	
Albertine (8% × 8,000)	640	
		(6,960)
		50,000
Balance of profit shared in profit sharing ratio		
Geoffrey 6/10	30,000	
Victoria 3/10	15,000	
Albertine 1/10	5,000	
		50,000

ORDER FORM

Any books from our AAT range can be ordered by telephoning 020-8740-2211. Alternatively, send this page to our Freepost address or fax it to us on 020-8740-1184, or email us at **publishing@bpp.com**. Or look us up on our Website: www.bpp.com.

We aim to deliver to all UK addresses inside 5 working days; a signature will be required. Orders to all EI addresses should be delivered within 6 working days. All other orders to overseas addresses should be delivered within 8 working days.

To: BPP Publishing Ltd, Aldine House, Aldine Place, London W12 8AW

Tel: 020-8740-2211   **Fax: 020-8740-1184**   **Email: publishing@bpp.com**

Mr / Ms (full name): _____

Day-time delivery address: _____

_____

Postcode: _____   Daytime Tel: (for queries only):_____

Please send me the following quantities of books:

	5/00 Interactive text	8/00 DA Kit	8/00 CA Kit
FOUNDATION			
Unit 1 Recording Income and Receipts	☐	☐	
Unit 2 Making and Recording Payments	☐	☐	
Unit 3 Ledger Balances and Initial Trial Balance	☐		☐
Unit 4 Supplying Information for Management Control	☐	☐	
Unit 20 Working with Information Technology (8/00 Text)	☐		
Unit 22/23 Achieving Personal Effectiveness	☐		
INTERMEDIATE			
Unit 5 Financial Records and Accounts	☐		☐
Unit 6 Cost Information	☐		
Unit 7 Reports and Returns	☐	☐	
Unit 21 Information Technology	☐		
Unit 22: see below			
TECHNICIAN			
Unit 8/9 Core Managing Costs and Allocating Resources	☐		☐
Unit 10 Core Managing Accounting Systems	☐		
Unit 11 Option Financial Statements (Accounting Practice)	☐		☐
Unit 12 Option Financial Statements (Central Government)	☐	☐	
Unit 15 Option Cash Management and Credit Control	☐	☐	
Unit 16 Option Evaluating Activities	☐	☐	
Unit 17 Option Implementing Auditing Procedures	☐	☐	
Unit 18 Option Business Tax FA00 (8/00 Text)	☐		
Unit 19 Option Personal Tax FA00 (8/00 Text)	☐		
TECHNICIAN 1999			
Unit 17 Option Business Tax Computations FA99 (8/99 Text & Kit)	☐	☐	
Unit 18 Option Personal Tax Computations FA99 (8/99 Text & Kit)	☐	☐	
TOTAL BOOKS	☐ +	☐ +	☐ = ☐

@ £9.95 each = £ _____

Postage and packaging:

UK: £2.00 for each book to maximum of £10

Europe (inc ROI and Channel Islands): £4.00 for first book, £2.00 for each extra

Rest of the World: £20.00 for first book, £10 for each extra

P & P £ _____

➤ Unit 22 Maintaining a Healthy Workplace Interactive Text (postage free) ☐ @ £3.95 £ _____

GRAND TOTAL £ _____

I enclose a cheque for £ _____ (cheques to **BPP Publishing Ltd**) or charge to **Mastercard/Visa/Switch**

Card number ☐☐☐☐ ☐☐☐☐ ☐☐☐☐ ☐☐☐☐ ☐☐☐☐ ☐☐☐☐

Start date _____ _____   Expiry date _____   Issue no. (Switch only)___

Signature _____

REVIEW FORM & FREE PRIZE DRAW

All original review forms from the entire BPP range, completed with genuine comments, will be entered into one of two draws on 31 January 2001 and 31 July 2001. The names on the first four forms picked out on each occasion will be sent a cheque for £50.

Name: _____   Address: _____

_____

_____

How have you used this Central Assessment Kit?
(Tick one box only)

☐ Home study (book only)

☐ On a course: college _____

☐ With 'correspondence' package

☐ Other _____

Why did you decide to purchase this Central Assessment Kit? *(Tick one box only)*

☐ Have used BPP Texts in the past

☐ Recommendation by friend/colleague

☐ Recommendation by a lecturer at college

☐ Saw advertising

☐ Other _____

During the past six months do you recall seeing/receiving any of the following?
(Tick as many boxes as are relevant)

☐ Our advertisement in *Accounting Technician* magazine

☐ Our advertisement in *Pass*

☐ Our brochure with a letter through the post

Which (if any) aspects of our advertising do you find useful?
(Tick as many boxes as are relevant)

☐ Prices and publication dates of new editions

☐ Information on Interactive Text content

☐ Facility to order books off-the-page

☐ None of the above

Have you used the companion Interactive Text for this subject?   ☐ Yes   ☐ No

Your ratings, comments and suggestions would be appreciated on the following areas

	Very useful	Useful	Not useful
Introductory section (How to use this Central Assessment Kit etc)	☐	☐	☐
Practice Questions	☐	☐	☐
Central Assessment Style Questions	☐	☐	☐
December 1999 Central Assessment	☐	☐	☐
Content of Answers	☐	☐	☐
Layout of pages	☐	☐	☐
Structure of book and ease of use	☐	☐	☐

	Excellent	Good	Adequate	Poor
Overall opinion of this Kit	☐	☐	☐	☐

Do you intend to continue using BPP Assessment Kits/Interactive Texts/? ☐ Yes   ☐ No

Please note any further comments and suggestions/errors on the reverse of this page.

Please return to: Nick Weller, BPP Publishing Ltd, FREEPOST, London, W12 8BR

REVIEW FORM & FREE PRIZE DRAW (continued)

Please note any further comments and suggestions/errors below

FREE PRIZE DRAW RULES

1   Closing date for 31 January 2001 draw is 31 December 2000. Closing date for 31 July 2001 draw is 30 June 2001.

2   Restricted to entries with UK and Eire addresses only. BPP employees, their families and business associates are excluded.

3   No purchase necessary. Entry forms are available upon request from BPP Publishing. No more than one entry per title, per person. Draw restricted to persons aged 16 and over.

4   Winners will be notified by post and receive their cheques not later than 6 weeks after the relevant draw date.

5   The decision of the promoter in all matters is final and binding. No correspondence will be entered into.